THE ARCHITECTURE OF ALDEN B. DOW

"Gardens never end and buildings never begin."

The Architecture of ALDEN B. DOW

SIDNEY K. ROBINSON

Wayne State University Press / Detroit

03   02   01   00   6   5   4   3

Library of Congress Cataloging in Publication Data

Robinson, Sidney K., 1943–
   The architecture of Alden B. Dow.

   Bibliography: p.
   Includes index.
   1. Dow, Alden B., 1904–   . 2. Midland (Mich.)—
Buildings.   3. Architecture, Modern—20th century—
United States.   I. Title.
   NA737.D67R6   1983   720′.92′4   82–24737
   ISBN 0–8143–1720–0 (cloth)
   ISBN 0–8143–1721–9 (pbk.)

This book was brought to publication with the assistance
of a grant from the Michigan Council for the Arts.

Photographic Credits

All photographs not listed below are from the files of Alden B.
Dow Associates Architects and are reproduced by permission.

Elmer L. Astleford, Figures 23, 24, 26, 30, 34, 37, 39, 45, 46, 47,
   48, 50, 51, 57, 60, 62, 63, 64, 66, 68, 71, 77, 78, 79, 81, 82, 85,
   86, 88, 89, 124
Daniel Bartush, Figures 95, 128, 130
Beutel, Figure 43
Gerald Gard, Figures 96, 98, 102, 105, 122, 127
Hedrich-Blessing, Figures 107, 108, 109, 110, 111, 112, 114, 118,
   123, 126
Myron Johnson, Figure 103
Balthazar Korab, Figures 1, 106
Douglas Lyttle, Figure 115
Sidney K. Robinson, Figures 2, 11, 12, 17, 25, 69, 70, 87, 94, 131
R. W. Tebbs, Figures 6, 7
R. Thomas, Figures 8, 10, 14, 15, 16, 18, 19, 20, 22, 32, 33, 52,
   53, 54, 55, 74, 76, 90, 100, 101
William Vandivert, Figures 3, 59, 125
Weiner, Figures 21, 99
Wright, Figure 21

Contents

Preface

Some buildings are famous because they are large. Others are famous because they were first: their style or structure or function set a pattern that others followed. Some buildings are famous because they are simple, others because they are complex. Alden B. Dow's architecture is outstanding because it is the emblem of a place, a time, and a man. The place is Midland, Michigan, a small town that is headquarters for a multinational chemical company. The time is the middle of our century. The man is Dow himself, an architect who has produced buildings both rare and indigenous—indigenous because Dow's greatest successes are domestic environments for people who are independent and self-reliant judges of aesthetic experience, rare because Dow has had an unusual opportunity to execute his and his clients' aesthetic intentions free of the necessity to compromise.

Dow's architecture received national attention from the first, in part because he was identified with Frank Lloyd Wright. Professional journals of the 1930s viewed his work against the background of Wright's and of European modernism. Talbot Hamlin's commentary on Dow's buildings in 1941 placed them close to the line dividing these two schools of architecture, praising them when they tended to follow European models, criticizing them when they displayed what Hamlin saw as Wrightian "exaggerations."

Once the debate over the direction of modern architecture in America had passed, Dow's work was noticed less frequently. His career provides a case study of an architect finding his own place among contending forces. He was born on April 10, 1904. From early childhood he wanted to become an architect (he remembers creating ground plans on the lawn of his father's house with rooms outlined in fallen leaves). He began his university studies in chemical engineering but soon transferred his attention to architecture. He was graduated from the Columbia University School of Architecture in 1931, and there acquired an American Beaux Arts training based on a tradition of composition in accordance with changing technological capabilities.

After working for several months with Frank Lloyd Wright at Taliesin in the summer of 1933, Dow returned to Midland and became the first Taliesin Fellow to build on his own. What he built first were outstanding private houses, most of them in Midland. As the son of the founder of Dow Chemical, he found a ready-made clientele for his domestic housing among its managers. The first public statement of his design philosophy was made in a talk in January, 1934, while he was at work on his own studio (Fig. 1), a striking example of the English eighteenth-century "Picturesque" tradition. Even today, when Dow stands on a low rise and looks across the pond to this building, he sees it as a "beautiful picture." It is not an epic canvas but a composition at the scale of the individual observer.

Figure 1. Alden Dow's studio, Midland, 1934–37. When the residence was added in 1941, a setting for working and living in a garden was complete.

From 1930 to 1950 Dow's work reflected the influence of Wrightian organic architecture and the "modernism" of the thirties. After 1950 his office produced more and more larger buildings—churches, offices, and schools. Today he discusses his architecture in terms of "composed order," by which he means a balance of subjective and objective forces, a harmony of sensory contrasts, a unity of fact and feeling. Composed order seeks to unite picturesque and social requirements in a comprehensive way. Dow's views on architecture express an uncomplicated aesthetic, an unruffled faith in individual effort. A simplified building program embodies those views most effectively.

Dow's thought has doubtless remained uncomplicated because he has not had to respond to pressing challenges in his daily work. His family's social and economic preeminence in the small town of Midland created a private and privileged world around him. From childhood his life has been protected by the fruits of his father's tough-minded technical and business operations, and because the tough-mindedness required to overcome adversity was unnecessary for Alden, it has always been uncongenial to him. In fact, from his father, one could say that Dow received the gift described by John Adams in 1780: "I must study politics and war, that my sons may have liberty to study . . . commerce and agriculture . . . in order to give to their children a right to study painting, poetry, music and architecture."[1] His clients' relations with Dow have always been characterized by deference on their part. An architect in such a position, it is thought, "bestows" designs much as one bestows gifts, and the recipient is grateful and appreciative. In Dow's case this deferential attitude is not always confined to family, friends, and clients. For example, when *Architectural Record* reviewed the fifty years of American architecture from 1891 to 1941, and discussed the George Greene house, it referred to the designer as "Mr. Dow," the only architect to whom it showed such formality.

My association with Alden Dow began when I visited Midland in January of 1959 to see the Frank Lloyd Wright exhibit put together by members of Dow's staff. The trip included a visit to Dow's studio. As a sixteen-year-old I was captivated by that low green-and-white structure spreading out over the snow. Eleven years later I was hired as junior designer in Dow's office. In 1974 I completed my doctoral dissertation on Wright's Taliesin and Dow's Studio, and four years later the Michigan Society of Architects asked me to prepare a monograph on Dow's career. This book has been written with his help. He has made available his drawings and project files, and I have also gathered together here, along with the descriptions of completed buildings, plans, and photographs, Dow's thoughts on architecture and its purpose.

Note

1. *Letters of John Adams to His Wife*, ed. Charles Francis Adams, 1841 edition, vol. 2, letter 78.

Acknowledgments

Without the assistance and trust of Alden Dow, this monograph would not have been produced. I thank him for his generous guidance. Bill Gilmore, Jim Howell, and Dick Schell of his staff were most helpful, and Sara Paulsen, Bernie Rahn, Bev Grubb, and Cliff Amrhein assisted in countless ways. Nancy Barker's bibliographic research for the 1974 exhibit of Dow's work at the Midland Center for the Arts was most useful in compiling the Bibliography.

The Michigan Society of Architects deserves commendation and thanks for the time and effort given by the Executive Board, President John Jickling, and the Editorial Board, chaired initially by Denis Schmiedeke and subsequently by Harry Van Dine. Ann Stacy, the Executive Director, was patient and supportive. The idea of an M.S.A. publications program originated with Denis Schmiedeke, who dedicated himself to this endeavor. Robert Bell drew upon his years with Dow's office to make timely suggestions, and his assistance is gratefully acknowledged.

The dating of the buildings given in text and figure legends represents the earliest appearance in the project drawings of the version actually constructed.

THE ARCHITECTURE OF ALDEN B. DOW

1. Early Experiences and First Designs

Alden Dow's first memorable encounter with architecture was in January, 1923. He was eighteen and at the Imperial Hotel in Tokyo on a trip with his family when he was overwhelmed by the ornamental richness and spatial complexity lavished by Frank Lloyd Wright on the building. Dow's father also loved the hotel and several years later suggested that Alden make two lanterns like those standing at its entrance, based on published photographs of them. The construction of these large, pierced spheres supported by two intersecting fins proved to be a greater challenge than even a magnesite cement developed by the Dow Chemical Company could meet. As an alternative, with the help of a German craftsman and the available cement, Alden carved a nymph like one designed by Wright and Alfonso Iannelli that he had seen in photographs of Wright's Midway Gardens. (The sculpture now stands on a hill in the Dow gardens behind the family house [Fig. 2].) Japan's traditional culture so engaged Alden's interest that on his return from Japan he exhibited a tray garden at the Midland Garden Club.

Following in the steps of his older brother Willard, Alden entered the University of Michigan to become a chemical engineer, in the family tradition. After two years, the fact that most of his friends seemed to be in the U. of M. architecture school indicates where his heart lay. He left the university and, after working for a year at the Dow plant back in Midland, announced to his parents one morning that he wanted to study architecture at Columbia University in New York City.

Columbia's Beaux Arts program under William A. Boring began its students' education with such courses as "The Elements of Architecture," "The Orders and Their Application," "Shades and Shadows," and the history of Greek and Roman architecture. The most important field of instruction, design, included history, drawing (no less than four hours a week), graphics, mathematics, and construction. Competitive problems in the design course were solved both in drawings and models.[1] When Dow arrived all the faculty were known for adherence to solid, traditional principles. In 1930 Lemuel C. Dillenback was brought to Columbia with the apparent intention of directing design students toward prizes. His students remember that his concerns lay less in construction than in the strength of the plan drawing. Joseph Hudnut's broad understanding of the history of architecture, both ancient and modern, helped set the tone for his students.

In the summer of 1929 Dow and two classmates made a grand tour of Europe and visited the major architectural sites on the Continent after a brief visit to England. Dow took photographs while the others recorded French cathedrals, Carcassonne, the Mediterranean, Florence, and Venice in watercolors. They went to Vienna, then on to

Munich, Heidelberg, and Rothenburg, and visited some of the new brick housing in Amsterdam.

Back at school in New York, Dow could see many new buildings whose designs reflected the effect of the 1925 Paris Exposition of Decorative Arts. The Weiner Werkstätte Gallery was on Fifth Avenue, and things Parisian were everywhere. Interiors were paneled in wood veneer or brightened by highly colored patterned fabrics, paint, and linoleum. The new look in decorative objects could be more easily understood in terms of design elements than in terms of traditional styles. Abroad Dow had acquired numerous French and German publications on the new architecture and interior design.[2] Even in the American architectural press the Bauhaus was known, but its abrupt departures from what had gone before were often considered unnecessarily harsh, though some of Gropius' minimal houses demonstrating new modular construction techniques were appreciated for their ingenuity, if not for their architectural composition. The work of Joseph Urban, with his background in the Vienna Secession, was more accessible. In the late twenties and early thirties, his mirrored ceilings for the Central Park Casino, extended staging to skirt the front seating areas in his New School for Social Research auditorium, and proposal for the Metropolitan Opera had attracted attention.

Paul Frankl, in his 1928 book *New Dimensions* (which was in Dow's library), and in *Form and Reform* of 1930, had presented an amalgam of Wright's organicism and European Style Moderne. A young man like Dow, from a newly successful business family, would naturally be responsive to moderately progressive design.

Dow's continuing interest in Wright led him to contact Taliesin in the spring of 1930 to ask whether he could come to work there. Wright replied: "I might take you if I liked you,"[3] and, after a meeting in May while Wright was giving his Princeton lectures, said that he would let Dow know when plans for the School of Allied Arts at Taliesin developed. As it turned out, Dow heard nothing further from Wright, and, upon graduation from Columbia in 1931, returned to Michigan to work for Frantz and Spence, a Saginaw firm.

The first commission Dow received was the clubhouse for the new Midland Country Club. The previous summer Herbert Dow had urged its directors to build a clubhouse for the golf course they had carved out of farmland four years before. By way of encouragement he presented his twenty-seven-year-old son's sketch for the building, which was accepted. On the title sheet of the 1930 working drawings Dow's initials are worked into the square logo he had adopted. The day before the building opened in May of the next year, the *Midland Republican* ran a fourteen-page special edition on this new "community house." Its buff-colored stucco covered a cinderblock structure that contained locker rooms, dining rooms, lounges, and thirteen guest rooms (Figs. 3–4). At the entrance a row of piers separated windows with square leading. The balcony over the doors was supported at the ends by stepped-profile brackets, echoed in the lampposts along the driveway. The locker room at the back, more slab-sided, was given continuous bands. This contrast with the geometric patterns at the front reflects two major choices available to a young designer in 1930: Style Moderne and what would shortly be labeled the International Style.

Dow was the chairman of the furnishings and decorations committee. Each of the four lounges, to the left and right of the entry and the mezzanine above, had a fireplace whose triangular patterns above the mantels pointed either up or down in the ancient representation of male and female. In the 36- by 46-foot dining room-ballroom, Dow created "rainbow lighting," of which he was particularly proud. Along three sides of the high ceiling ran a dropped panel edged in frosted glass with colored bulbs behind it, all controlled by switches and dimmers. In the middle of the floor a six- by twelve-foot heavy opalescent glass panel covered more colored lights, similarly controlled. This room, with its "Dowmetal" (magnesium) chairs and the reflections from the patterned windows, rivaled the St. George Hotel ballroom in Brooklyn of 1929, where Winhold Reiss had concealed colored cove lights controlled by buttons to alter the mood. The editorial in the special edition of the local newspaper was understandably proud: "There is something about Midland that differentiates it from other places, pleasingly and emphatically. This difference is to some extent intangible, but it is made up of tangible things that will be found to be permeated with a priceless community asset—love of the artistic." They adapted a slogan to express this attitude: "Not one cent for mediocrity, but thousands for an artistry that is unique."

Further tangible evidence of the city's artistic concerns were the unique county building (1925) designed by Cleveland architect Bloodgood Tuttle, with its scenic murals of ground glass in stucco by Paul Honoré, and the cash prizes awarded to attractive yards and gardens, for which Alden Dow served as judge the summer after his return from Japan. Herbert H. Dow was the leading force in these endeavors locally and state-wide as a trustee of the Michigan Art Institute. The new country club was only the latest triumph. In April, 1930, *Fortune Magazine* called attention to Midland's special role in showing how a great and modern industry could develop far from a metropolitan area, in a town which would demonstrate the American desire to balance country and city. The wilderness would be tamed, civilization would flourish.

The way Midland weathered the Depression reflects the unique stability of the place. In 1934 the chemical works had the highest employment ever, and to offset any sense of uncertainty, the company offered a $1,000 life insurance policy for any employee who wanted it. In addition, each employee could pay 84 cents a month for sickness and accident coverage. The five-day, forty-hour week went into effect in April, 1937, two months before the Dow stock was even listed on the New York Stock Exchange.

A serious housing shortage nationwide was aggravated in Midland by the few housing starts in the city.[4] The need for housing was recognized on a national level through Roosevelt's Better Housing Day in June, 1935, and nearer Midland the same concern

5

was evident in weekly fifteen-minute radio programs on house planning in the winter of 1935. The town's relative economic stability, need for new housing, and pride provided opportunities for a young architect. Almost all Dow's clients in his first five years came from among the members of the country club.

Dow's younger sister provided his first domestic commission, which he designed as an associate of Frantz and Spence. Margaret Dow was engaged to a medical student named Towsley, who was in school in Ann Arbor. The two planned to settle there and bought a lot. The preliminary plans of May, 1932 (Fig. 5), show a modest house with two bedrooms on the first floor and a study and bedroom in the basement, with the garage integrated into the plan. The contract for construction specified the three materials which dominate the composition: red common brick painted white, diamond-paned windows, and verdigris copper roof (Fig. 6). Vermilion gutters at the edge of the barely projecting roofs provide a color contrast. A passage behind a line of square brick piers links entry, kitchen, and garage. Dow's intention to keep the house low under the seamed roof was frustrated by the Ann Arbor building code, which required eight-foot ceilings throughout. After much argument, Dow raised the height, but he treated the incident with gentle humor by setting into the wall by the entrance, a series of ceramic plaques dramatizing the obstacles an architect encounters in achieving his plans. Interior wall surfaces were enlivened by painted brick and four-foot squares of Acoustex, whose texture Dow admired (Fig. 7), divided by battens of clear white birch that continue throughout the interior woodwork. The interiors are enriched at the ceiling by wood patterns over the hearth and along the diamond-paned windows. Lighting is concealed behind frosted glass over cabinet and fireplace. Although the exterior, with its hipped roof and broad chimney mass, may have some affinities with Wright's Oak Park work, its lack of overhangs and smoothly finished interiors are closer to examples of modern architecture then current.

In late 1934 Dow designed the first of several additions to the Towsley house. A bedroom and bath were built behind the garage, and a skylight was slipped into a fold in the new roof to light a raised conservatory and bathroom. New furnishings were approved by Dow from the Herman Miller line. Additional woodwork was supplied by Nachtagalls in Grand Rapids. Four years later a substantial enlargement along one side included two bedrooms, a master suite, and a screened porch, with a game room and maids' room below. In the later addition the building department allowed the lower ceilings. In 1960 the dining room was altered and a new diamond-paned front door was added.

Dow had not forgotten his conversation with Wright in 1930. In March, 1933, while working in Saginaw, though he had made plans to attend Cranbrook Academy of Art, outside Detroit, to work with Eliel Saarinen, he again contacted Wright at Taliesin about joining the Taliesin Fellowship. Wright replied that membership in the Fellowship was more than a job to which one commuted every day. Two years earlier Dow had married the daughter of one of his father's top executives, Vada Bennett, who would be accompanying him to this rural apprenticeship-fellowship and was not sure what she might be getting into. After reaching an understanding and paying the $450 fee, the Dows drove to Wisconsin that May. One day at Taliesin convinced them that they could indeed stay there.

As Edgar Tafel and others have related,[5] this first spring and summer at Taliesin were filled with adventure and struggle, as neglected buildings were refurbished and altered to accommodate the new inhabitants. In addition to building a stone pier, Dow took motion pictures of the daily chores, construction, and horseplay that filled that summer. Cushions had to be sewn, trees felled and cut up, and corn harvested. He recorded women in long dresses watching horses plowing the fields and scenes in the drafting room.

When he signed on as an apprentice at Taliesin, Dow brought a residential commission with him, a house in Midland for Earl Stein. A comparison of his drawings before he arrived there with the later versions made while working with Wright provides a rare chance to see how Dow's design preferences change as they approached, came in contact with, and passed beyond Wright's direct influence. Little more than a month after arriving at Taliesin, Dow was back in Michigan continuing discussions with his former Saginaw employers about arrangements for the Stein house. Stein, a division manager at the Dow plant and graduate of the Case School of Applied Science, became mayor of Midland a few years later after serving as alderman. Dow made an agreement to collaborate with Frantz and Spence on the house similar to that worked out for the Towsleys, in which he would be associate designer on the project.

When Dow returned to Taliesin in June, Wright convinced him to do the whole job of drawing up the Stein house through the Taliesin Fellowship. It was the first job to go through Wright's newly established apprentice system. On the last day of June Dow wrote Stein in Midland informing him of the change and reassuring him that dealing with an organization so new would not be risky. He himself would ensure that his first house in his home town would go up without a hitch:

> At present I am trying to get these sketches in shape for your final approval. Everyone here likes the house, including the very critical Mr. Wright. He has given me a number of criticisms which have resulted in definite improvements. I tried to develop the guest quarters over the garage but finally reached the conclusion that the added expense to make it look right was too great. It makes the garage appear much too high and important for the rest of the house. Now I am working on an idea of developing a sunken garden in the rear of the house in order to have circulation in the basement rooms, as we had them before. It is working out to be something very unusual and at-

tractive. It tends to spread the house out over a greater area by way of steps and low terrace walls. It also develops a very successful raised terrace as you suggested.[6]

Three weeks later Dow went back to Midland to go over the plans with the Steins and to sign a contract with them. But it was not until the end of September that sufficient progress had been made on the drawings to warrant another trip to present Stein with what Dow hoped would be "one of the best examples of modern architecture."[7]

The plan that he had taken to Taliesin (Fig. 8) was similar in materials and general appearance to the Towsley house of the previous year. A loggia of square brick piers led from garage to house. As in the Towsley house, the ribbed copper roof barely extended beyond the brick walls, which carried bands of steel casement windows. Though the Steins' large lot, bordering on a park, allowed free exposure on all sides, Dow's plan, like the roofs, was pulled tightly into itself. The symmetry of the major rooms was reinforced by a semicircular pool at the end of the dining room and a planting box opposite the fireplace in the living room. A garden next to the house was planned in a "French curve" pattern to contrast with the rectilinear forms of the house.

In response to the discussions at Taliesin, the character of the Stein house changed in several significant ways (Fig. 9). Extensive steps, terraces, and garden walls were extended from the house at 45- and 90-degree angles. Roof overhangs were extended to six feet and more (Fig. 10). The loggia piers, projected into three-and-a-half-foot fins, were continued past the garage and terminated in a tool room and parapet. The basic room arrangement was the same, but now wall and window areas were assymetrical, with the ends of the house stepped back at the corners under the wide overhangs (Fig. 11). The fireplace was no longer centered on the ridge of the plaster-hipped living room ceiling but tangent to it, and the copper fireplace hood was given a triangular pattern of battens (Fig. 12).

The interior finishes noted on the first plan included carpeted floors, plaster ceilings and walls, wood paneling, and Acoustex panels on walls and lowered soffits, all used in the Towsley house. The wood paneling of the first plan was eliminated in the Taliesin version, and the finish woodwork was to be straight grain cypress. White tile in the bathrooms contrasted with the brown fixtures in the master suite upstairs. The interior space was extended by replacing a solid wall between study and living room with a pattern of horizontal bands of varying lengths, produced by open cantilevered shelves. This functional-decorative feature also appeared in the lower game room here and with regularity in Dow's later houses.

The contract for construction was signed on October 30, 1933, and work began on the house the next day. From Wisconsin Dow kept in contact with the work through weekly reports from the superintendent, E. M. Tompkins, who was his site representative then and for some years afterward.

Dow clearly did not intend to stay very long at Taliesin. His periodic returns to Midland during the summer and fall, his wife's initial reluctance to stay at Taliesin, and the delivery of a letterhead for his Midland office in November indicate his desire to begin work on his own, though he later joked that he left Taliesin because he had had enough K.P. duty. By spending a few months with Wright, Dow was running the risk of being considered just another apprentice who wanted only to bask in Wright's reflected glory. That was the fate of those who joined the Fellowship in 1932–1933 and are still there. Others left after a few years, thoroughly saturated with organic architecture in its more easily grasped, decorative expression. The temptation to seize on the idiosyncrasies of Wright's designs, if indulged, could result in an over-literal understanding of his dictum of the continuity between the whole and the minutest part, the one expressing the other. From this it is an easy step to believe it possible to work up an architectural concept by means of sheer aggregation of detail.

Dow came to Taliesin somewhat resistant to Wrightian indoctrination because of his age (twenty-nine), his previous architectural training and executed commissions, his wide travel, and—on a practical level—his ability to begin building on his own immediately. He was not looking for an all-embracing answer to youthful questions. As noted earlier, he was the first Taliesin Fellow to go and build on his own, raising the fear in Wright's mind that he might be stolen from rather than being given the total allegiance he demanded. In fact, though Dow, along with many others, considered Wright's bravura style unnecessary, he did admire Wright's unit system and used it to organize his own designs. Wright had explored the expression of order, both in structure and appearance, through the use of a block system in his Arizona and California work in the twenties. From that unit system Dow developed his own simpler and more flexible "Unit Blocks." (Characteristically, Dow's block were not richly ornamented like Wright's.) In 1934 he told Wright how satisfying and challenging it was to design with the block but at the same time admitted that the frame wall, which was more flexible, should be developed further.[8]

The connection between Wright and Dow has often been made to seem simpler and more direct than is the case. For example, in February, 1936, Louis Untermeyer spoke in Midland on "The New American Arts." During the course of his talk he remarked, "I am amused to see Frank Lloyd Wright stuff done here in Midland skillfully and beautifully."[9] Dow's experience at Taliesin was well known. When he talked about architecture to groups in Midland, he used Wright's work as an example of forthright and beautiful design. Dow's chief draftsman, Robert Goodall, had worked with Wright in the early thirties at Taliesin, and Wright thought very highly of him. Because Dow had plenty of money and the services of such an assistant, Wright may have thought that he would be tempted to do things the easy way in architecture. Perhaps for this reason, he warned Dow, in a letter in the spring of 1937, that "facility is dangerous."[10] In April the *Midland Republican* announced that Wright would be giving a talk later in the month and that tickets would be available at Dow's office and from various civic groups. The day before the talk another story carried a photograph of Wright and the observation, "Midland houses reflect his themes." The report of the talk was headlined: "Wright Lauds Midland's Modernistic Homes: Architect Praises Dow." The story began:

> Frank Lloyd Wright, high priest of "Organic Architecture," last night acknowledged parentage of the Midland interpretation of his building theme and explained it as a "facing of Reality," and an abandoning of bogus culture. Wright, introduced by Alden B. Dow as "the one man who stands above all others in the history of architecture," named his former apprentice as "one of the nicest boys I've ever known," and tacitly accepted the architect's employment of his building theories as logical and authentic.[11]

Wright closed by describing Midland as an outpost of civilization.

Even when a building displayed virtually no "stylistic" traits at all, as in the Ingersoll demonstration home in Kalamazoo, *Interiors* commented in 1946: "Alden Dow still thinks like Frank Lloyd Wright."[12] When Columbia University held a symposium on modern architecture in 1961, Dow was invited to give the talk on the Wrightian tradition.[13] When a serious rift developed between the two architects in 1949 (details of this disagreement are given in Chapter 6 below), Dow tried to explain to Wright how one could learn from him without being dependent on him. Although Wright had set the direction for organic architecture, he said its vast implications could not be completely explored in one lifetime. Others would come along and add their contributions in a process of creative growth.[14]

Wright's Kaufmann house, Fallingwater, of 1936 can be seen as a response to contemporary European work, but his roots lay farther back in the Victorian era, while Dow, who began his career in the mid-twenties, never attempted Wright's complexity of expression. Wright seemed to enjoy being entangled in complications of form (as well as life pattern). His decorative propensities could run wild on those occasions when the client had sufficient funds and insufficient independence of mind. Dow was never so tempted. The stylishness he was exposed to in New York and its importance in the social circle in which he lived in Midland were never sacrificed to an aesthetic rigor which leaned toward discomfort. Carpeting and air-conditioning were present in most of Dow's houses from the beginning.

As we will see, Dow's philosophy of architecture was based on principles that Wright never mentioned. In some respects, his response to Wright was similar to that of Rudolph Schindler, who appreciated and understood Wright's construction and spatial ingenuity without falling victim to the philosophical and decorative entanglements that had trapped so many Taliesin apprentices. Walter Burley Griffin had also developed an individual architectural style after working with Wright from 1901 to 1905.

Some aspects of Griffin's theory, particularly regarding the individual's connection to the creative mind as the source of feelings rather than intellect,[15] have also been articulated by Dow. Dow's philosophical sources are American, not European, as are the Theosophy and Anthroposophy from which Griffin drew. And like others who worked with Wright, in 1934 Dow developed an architectural system of construction, the "Unit Blocks" mentioned earlier. Griffin's "Knitlock" system of 1917 was one of one-foot-square concrete tiles laid with steel and mortar; Rudolph Schindler experimented with modular poured concrete systems; and Barry Byrne developed a one-foot concrete unit system in 1933.[16]

Other American architects beginning to work in the thirties also developed architectural approaches that alternately emphasized European or American traditions. Two useful overviews of the range of available alternatives for private houses at the time are provided by *Architectural Forum*'s "50 New Houses" article in April, 1937, and the American Gas Association competition drawings in the *Forum*'s July, 1938, issue. In 1937 the houses shown are divided about equally between traditionalism and a modernism of two varieties: there are designs which closely adhere to a European "Internationalist" model, and others which dilute that importation with an indigenous tradition stemming from Wright. John Lloyd Wright's design for a house at Birchwood Beach is understandably the closest to his father's style, but even Schindler's McAlmon house in Los Angeles makes a rich, three-dimensional exercise out of the design as a whole.

The Gas Association competition entries also fall into the two categories of modernism. Some unite the two by means of a Wrightian plan expressed in severely planar elevations. The winner, designed by three Cranbrook students, is a compact house roofed in standing-rib metal. Although it is not obviously an imitation of Dow's work, its moderate and comfortable adjustment to the two streams of modern architecture is similar. Architects like Gregory Ain could also produce an effective blend, as in a house for Miss Urcel Daniel published in *Architectural Record* for February, 1940. Its sloped roofs and ceilings, dictated by deed restrictions, are cut away at the corners to expose rafter patterns. An ingenious recessed, mid-roof clerestory adds a functional and decorative feature to a house predominantly in the European mode. George Brigham in Ann Arbor, Michigan, Paul Schweikher in Chicago, and H. H. Harris in California developed distinctive American houses around 1940, but Dow's masterful examples—the Midland Country Club of 1930, reflecting New York fashions in modern architecture, the Towsley house of 1932, his personal amalgam of progressive metropolitan taste and Wrightian features, and the Stein house of 1933, directly influenced by Taliesin—came before them.

Notes

1. *Columbia University Bulletin of Information*, 29th ser., no. 2 (New York, 1929).

2. These publications included *Haus und Raum, Repertoire du Goût Moderne*, no. 2, and several issues of *Masters of the Colour Print*, published by *The Studio*.

3. Letter to Alden B. Dow, April 12, 1930. All personal letters cited in the notes are from the archives of Alden B. Dow Associates, Midland, Michigan, unless otherwise stated, and are used by permission.

4. *Midland Republican*, September 27, 1934.

5. Edgar Tafel, *Apprentice to Genius* (New York, 1979).

6. Letter to Earl Stein, June 30, 1933.

7. Letter to Earl Stein, September 19, 1933.

8. Letter to Frank Lloyd Wright in 1934.

9. Quoted in *Midland Republican*, February 6, 1936, p. 1.

10. Letter to Alden B. Dow, April, 1937.

11. *Midland Republican*, May 1, 1937, p. 1.

12. "Eight Men on a Unit," *Interiors*, May, 1946, pp. 86–87.

13. Alden B. Dow, "The Continuity of Idea and Form," in *Four Great Makers of Modern Architecture* (New York, 1961), pp. 24–26. Dow referred to unfolding space, the unit system, and the importance of the ends and beginnings of compositions.

14. Letter to Frank Lloyd Wright, February 7, 1949.

15. See Walter Burley Griffin, "Building for Nature," quoted in Donald Leslie Johnson, *The Architecture of Walter Burley Griffin* (South Melbourne, 1977), pp. 150–52. The article was originally published in *Advance! Australia IV* in March, 1928.

16. For the "Knitlock" system, see Johnson, *Griffin*, p. 56–60. Schindler's drawings of 1923 are illustrated in "Houses for Outdoor Life," *Architectural Record*, July, 1930, pp. 17–21. Byrne's system is discussed in *ibid.*, January, 1934, p. 31.

Early Experiences and First Designs / ILLUSTRATIONS

Early Experiences and First Designs

Nymph, Dow gardens, Midland, ca. 1926. Dow modeled this sculpture after one by Alfonso Iannelli and Frank Lloyd Wright in the Midway Gardens in Chicago.

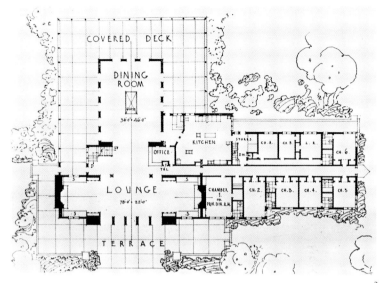

Midland Country Club, Midland, 1930. Dow designed this clubhouse while he was a student of architecture at Columbia University. Its interior is ornamented with colored lights and geometric patterns in plaster, wood, and glass.

3

4

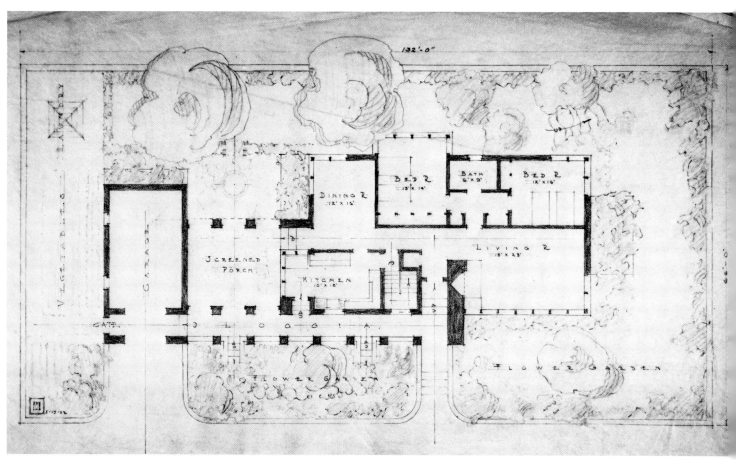

5

Harry and Margaret Towsley house, Ann Arbor, 1932. The preliminary plan (Fig. 5) shows how this compact house integrates the garage into the composition. The luxurious plantings which screen the house complement the broad planes of roof, windows, and brick. The highly finished wood ornament above the windows and fireplace (Fig. 7) contrasts with rougher wall textures of painted brick and Acoustex panels. Lights are concealed behind frosted glass atop the cabinet and at the ceiling above the fireplace.

6

7

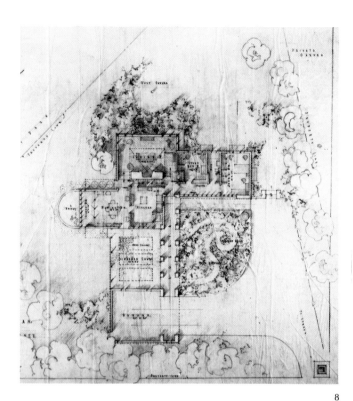

8

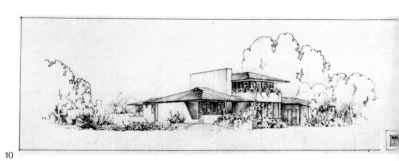

10

Earl Stein house, Midland, 1933. Dow took this plan (Fig. 8) to Taliesin when *went there to study. The materials and general appearance of this version of th*
Stein house recall the Towsley house of the previous year. The revised plan (F
9), redrawn in fall 1933 under Wright's direct influence, breaks the tightly co
tained perimeter to allow the house to extend into the landscape. In the perspe
tive view (Fig. 10) the effect of the plan extensions are visible in the exterior as te
races and cantilevered roofs project from the body of the house.

Today the living room of the Stein house retains the contrast of the ornamented copper fireplace hood and brick with smooth plaster surfaces, of
high ceilings with low, and of solid walls with broad window areas.

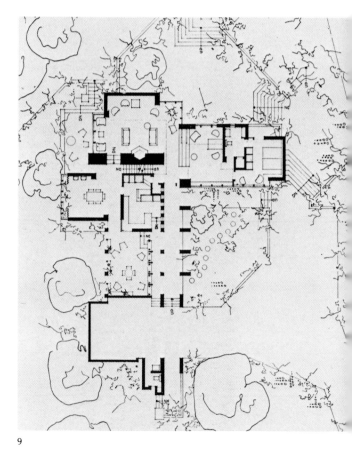

12   9

Copper in the roof and wall panels link the master bedroom windows to the dining room windows below (Fig. 11). Dow kept the house low, as Figure 13 indicates, by opening the lower bedrooms and sitting room onto a sunken garden, much as he had done in the Towsley house. A glazed triangle in the roof lets in light above the hearth.

11

2. Alden Dow's Studio

When Alden Dow's name is attached to a published building, it is most likely to be a picture of his studio in Midland, Michigan. A green-and-white structure overlooking a pond, interwoven with water and luxuriant vegetation, it is visual poetry composed of contrasts of color, line, and plane. This personal building serves as a touchstone for Dow's subsequent work. It was not the first building he built after leaving Taliesin, but the intention to create his own studio must surely have been stimulated by seeing the home and studio Wright had made for himself.

On his return to Midland, he set up a temporary office in the home of his brother-in-law, Dr. William Hale, a widower who was living in Washington, D.C., with his daughter at the time. During the winter of 1933–1934, Dow looked for a site along one of the several streams running through the family property west of town. Along one of them he found a large maple tree that could be incorporated into a composition of building and nature. The studies for a studio at this location evolved from the rectilinear geometry of the Unit Blocks which Dow had been working on for a year. In them, two long, low, pergola-like wings meet in a right angle near the tree. At the corner they pile up in a higher assembly of blocks topped by thin planes and edged by patterned windows (Figs. 14–15).

For all the beauties of the site, its lack of utility connections was an insurmountable drawback. When he found how long it would take to get the necessary hookups made, Dow realized that he must find a more convenient location. To the west of his father's garden, a small stream flowed by a plum and apple orchard. His father had pursued pomiculture very seriously and at one time intended to collect every kind of plum he could. The orchard was at the end of a short street already served by utilities. Extending them a couple of hundred feet would not be difficult. When the location was settled, a temporary structure was erected, as the Hales were returning to their house for the summer and Dow needed work space immediately. In a matter of weeks, a wood and masonite "railroad car," as Dow called it, went up along the ditch. The common-sense simplicity evident throughout its panel and wood framework construction (Figs. 16–17) reappears periodically in Dow's experiments with inexpensive housing.

During the fall of 1934 and winter of 1935, plans and details for expanding the entrance, roofing with sheet copper, and embedding a conference room in the pond were well along. Construction and design could proceed together with an office staff that included carpenters and laborers as well as draftsmen. The studio remains the only example of concrete Unit Blocks combined with sloped sheltering roofs: the first Unit Block houses later built in Midland are closer in basic form to the sketches of the studio which were made for the first, more remote, site.

Dow developed his Unit Blocks, which he patented in 1936, as a way of constructing walls and openings in satisfying alignment and of creating textural interest. Before he went to Taliesin he had been working on a cubic block of concrete. The possible variations of a wall laid up with these cubes was limited, and it was not structurally very solid. Upon returning to Midland, Dow tried to find a form that would be free of these drawbacks. The solution, first modeled in wood, was a block whose exposed faces were one foot square but whose plan was a forty-five-degree rhombus (Fig. 18). The variations suggested by this angled form and the offset joints from course to course were exactly what Dow was looking for. The full-size blocks were cast from cinder concrete in sixteen different shapes (Fig. 19). Although Dow did not rely exclusively on this material for walls, it became a distinctive feature in his early work.

Plans for expanding the studio were determined in part by the need to create a satisfying termination to the long drafting-room roof. A pencil drawing in color of three elevations (Fig. 20) shows an almost perverse relation of the sunken conference room to the water: the copper of the roof is brought down the walls of the room and ends a foot above the water level; there a narrow band of windows permits an abrupt closeup view of the pond. A line sketched over the elevation gives the final roof configuration: a hipped-roof form spreads to a level eaveline five feet above the water. The roof and the windows create an arrow-like shape, symmetrical about the diagonal ridge line, broken at one point by a "kite" window looking back along the drafting room (Fig. 21). Dow made small plasticene models as well as drawings to study the form of the roof and the composition as a whole (Figs. 22–23).

By the end of 1935, some twenty thousand dollars had been spent creating this pond-side studio. It had a multiplicity of uses: the Dows used it as an evening sitting room when they were living in the last house on the street leading to the studio. It even served as the setting for the marriage of Mrs. Dow's sister, Grace, when a string quartet played in the lowest room, by the water, and the ceremony took place in front of a fire in the upper reception space, filled with ferns and palm leaves.

Dow could easily check the effect of the design, as the construction was proceeding at his front door. Carpenters and masons, however, were not constantly faced with revised plans, since Dow believed that one should mean what one drew. He did make one adjustment, however, after he looked at the construction from his father's garden across the stream. As the drafting-room wall was prepared for the application of a continuous stucco surface, Dow noticed the rectilinear pattern of the framing and decided to preserve the effect by breaking up the plaster surface into panels. In the soffit, or underside of the roof overhanging this wall, horizontal windows are placed to give views down to the water.

In 1934 Dow put up what he called a "shanty" for himself and his wife in the orchard to the north of the office. It was a quickly built shelter with a large hearth. When he was showing a friend its progress, he asked the carpenter how long he had been at work on it, with the intent of showing his friend how quickly the structure was going up. The carpenter took the question as a criticism, packed up, and left the site.

Dow went to the man's house to explain and ask him to return, but to no avail. The goodwill of the craftsmen on his jobs was very important to Dow after this incident, and he took pains to keep it.

In November of 1936 a horse team began excavating for another studio space, at right angles to the initial drafting room, much like the arrangement for the initial site. The new space ended at the north with the garage, shop, and heating plant for the growing complex. In contrast to the simple roof of the original drafting room, the new studio space, partly sunk into the ground, had large triangular windows cut into the northeast side of an elaborately folded roof.

By the summer of 1937 the studio was complete. The pond itself had been created a year earlier by damming downstream, and the plantings were in place. On the pond-side were pines, birches, spruce, willows, and wisteria; in the water, cattails and lilies (Fig. 24). Standing on a low rise looking down on the building from across the pond, Dow says today, "Isn't that a beautiful picture?" The lines made by the bevels in the square blocks and the standing seams of the roof contrast with the foliage, and all is re-flected and softened in the still surface of the pond. The view from above, from the shade of the trees out and down to the structure in full sunlight below, is strangely un-real. Looking down on a building is a way to remove it from our normal relationship with man-made structures, and we are further disoriented because we are not quite sure how big it is. The windows by which we judge size are at the water level, where the roof is only five feet high. If the roof is normal height, the building must be farther away than we think. A door and other windows partially visible in this view are cam-ouflaged under the roof. The ambiguity of our spatial relation to this view is a major part of its fascination.

The straight and irregular lines, white blocks and green roof, and textured and smooth surfaces are brought together in an abstract visual composition. The blocks are pavement, stepping stones, and walls. They are part of the building, part of the ground, and part of the water (Fig. 25). In one configuration, they make a stalagmite form which hides the chimney. The planar surface of the pond is set against circular tanks and square pads visible just below the water and the blocks above the water.

While Dow was creating his studio, Wright was ruminating over his design for the Kaufmann house at Bear Run. Both Norris K. Smith and Martin Engel have remarked on the ambiguous effect of the abstract elements comprising Fallingwater.[1] In Dow's scheme the relation is more complex because the architect has composed both site and building, confounding even further the nature-construction distinction. Here the white blocks are analogous to a crystalline rock outcrop along the stream, a perfect place to set up camp in the woods. This "rationalized nature" is uncovered and a por-tion of it used as a firm base for the structure. Three rows of blocks, some hundred feet from the building, are imbedded in the very hill which provides the perfect pictur-esque view. Their placement, far from any structure, carries through the geological analogy. This stretched-out form along still water seems a more complete expression of the lyrical tradition of the picturesque than the gravity-defying leap halfway across a waterfall in Pennsylvania.

The picturesque is indeed like a picture, a moment in time captured and composed by the artist. Our relation to the scene is controlled insofar as a viewpoint is carefully selected for proper visual effect. Two leading advocates of the picturesque mode of seeing and designing were Uvedale Price (1747–1829) and Richard Payne Knight (1750–1824). At the beginning of the nineteenth century, they engaged in a public discussion of the characteristics common to painting, landscape gardening, and domestic architecture.[2] They each inherited an estate in the western counties of England, which they improved in the new mode of planned irregularity. The two men were not of old aristocratic stock but had acquired the refined taste suitable to such a position. They believed that nature, buildings, and paintings should all present abrupt variations, roughness, and irregularity. Buildings should fit in or respond to their natural locations through a judicious balance of harmony and contrast. Picturesque aesthetic theory was limited to houses in some sort of landscape setting. In general, Price and Knight wished to provide sensory stimulation to a contemporary aesthetic based on classical models that lacked sufficient visual contrast. One of the curiosities of the building-site relationship in early picturesque theory is the relative unimportance placed on the view *from* the house as compared to the view *of* the house. For Knight, a proper building required a controlled viewpoint.[3] The familiar picturesque view of Fallingwater can be gained only after a difficult descent down its rocky stream. Alden Dow concealed his studio from public view, but a short stroll around the pond brings the viewer to the slight but strategically located elevation affording the perfect view.

The plan of the studio matches its appearance; it is allowed to wander freely along the water's edge and among the trees. It is the most freely disposed of any of Dow's buildings, not only in its three-dimensional effect but in the interest of "plan appeal." Dow admits that this plan was in part determined by his attempt to create a satisfying composition of abstract forms which would obey the same principle of contrast as its textural, spatial, and coloristic dimensions. When Dow applies this principle, and when the building's parts are not too varied, or repetitious, or large, his plans, volumes, textures, colors, and landscaping, separately and together, illustrate the power of picturesque or scenographic design.

The conscious arrangement of visual relations within the scene is not intended to be "natural," but aesthetic. Price and Knight had struggled with the problem of differing temporal components in the aesthetic experience of painting, landscape, and buildings. In literature, as Joseph Frank has pointed out,[4] a "frozen moment" is characteristic of the literary form called the lyric, in which the decay of time is arrested through description and emotion. The lyric that looks at man in nature of course is the pastoral, an ancient tradition full of beauty and charm.

The view of Dow's studio is the purest form of lyrical artifice, a pastoral. The geology is manufactured, the trees have all been carefully planted, and the pond waters are controlled by a dam which prevents flooding of the pondside room. An extensive cottage, the studio seems to be living below its means in the interest of poetry. Such artifice is successful only if the means to carry out a picturesque composition are available, and one of its requirements is space. Price, Knight, and Dow were all able to build such complete compositions.

A curious feature of a three-dimensional picturesque view is that one can enter the composition and look back at the viewpoint. From inside the conference room of the studio, the pond appears much smaller and the opposite bank disturbingly close, which may explain why some later Dow houses look quite different in front and in back. The interior achieves a compositional balance only when its visual complexity is mentally compared to the underlying geometric order. At first glance its variations in surface, sloped and folded roofs, and square walls and hearth may seem too agitated. With further contact and the discovery of the underlying visual and structural order, the picturesque balance is restored. The arrival at the almost symmetrical pondside room (enlivened by watery reflections on its ceiling) comes as a calm conclusion to an exciting descent from the front door.

In addition to the immediate sensory experience, one may see something distinctly oriental, specifically Japanese (the perfection of the Katsura Detached Palace outside Kyoto comes to mind) in the studio view. The small size and the relation between construction and nature contribute to this impression, but the stepping stones and foliage are the most striking parallels. In the nineteenth century, Japan presented an aesthetic culture of charmingly composed objects and picturesque views. Mists framed objects both natural and architectural. Food, trinkets, fabrics, wood-block prints—all seemed "composed" for the effect. Japan seemed to be a magic place where time stood still. Its handicrafts were embraced by those who saw in them an escape from the violent disruptions of an industrial society, though others rejected them for their superficial prettiness. The small scale of the country and its people and their self-effacing manner struck Western realists as lacking masculine vigor. Its exotic architecture was classified as "non-historical" by Banister Fletcher in his *History of Architecture on the Comparative Method,*[5] but it suggested possibilities periodically forgotten in the West. Dow's love of Japan, in part stimulated by his father's interest, his visit there as a boy, and his enjoyment of Okakura Kakuzo's *Book of Tea,* and Lafcadio Hearn's stories lie behind the design of his studio.

The atmosphere of repose of the studio, noticed both by visitors and by people who work there every day, has fascinated photographers of every sort. Employees over the years have lovingly recorded each feature, and Dow himself has produced a beautiful movie of it as it lives through the changing seasons. It is a perfect demonstration of composed visual contrasts as it moves through the sequence of seasonal colors and textures. But beyond the visual appeal, the studio is probably the most striking embodiment of the general principles of architecture with which Dow works.

Notes

1. Norris Kelley Smith, *Frank Lloyd Wright* (Englewood Cliffs, N.J., 1966); Martin Engel, "The Ambiguity of Frank Lloyd Wright: Fallingwater," *The Charette*, April, 1964, pp. 17–18.

2. See Uvedale Price, *On the Picturesque* (Edinburgh, 1794); Richard Payne Knight, *An Analytical Inquiry into the Principles of Taste* (London, 1808), and *The Landscape: A Didactic Poem* (London, 1795). For modern commentary on the concept, see Peter Collins, *Changing Ideals in Modern Architecture* (Montreal, 1967), ch. 3; Christopher Hussey, *The Picturesque* (London, 1962); and Geoffrey Scott, *The Architecture of Humanism*, 2d ed. (Garden City, N.Y., 1924), ch. 3.

3. Knight, *Analytical Inquiry*, 4th ed. (Hants., England, 1972), p. 225.

4. Joseph Frank, "Spatial Form in Modern Literature," in *The Widening Gyre* (New Brunswick, N.J., 1963), pp. 3–62.

5. See the 8th ed. (New York, 1929), pt. 2, "The Non-Historical Styles."

Alden Dow's Studio / ILLUSTRATIONS

Alden Dow's Studio

These two drawings made in 1934, the one above by Dow's chief draftsman, Robert Goodall, and the one below by Dow himself, show the initial studio site farther from town. The elevations show the large maple tree integrated into the composition and the unique appearance of Dow's Unit Blocks oriented diagonally in the bridge to the left.

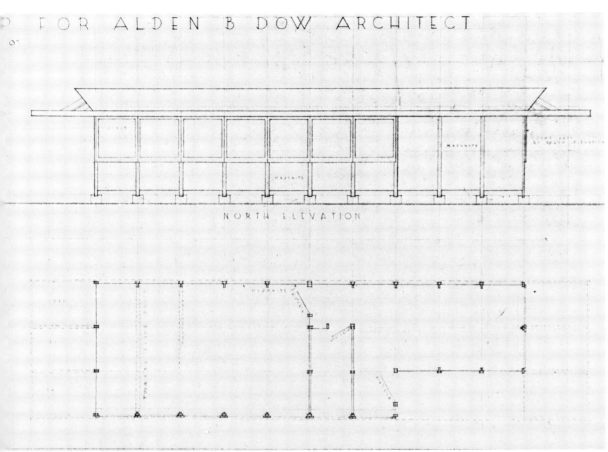

NORTH ELEVATION

16

udio drafting room plan. This simple structure
f wood frame and asbestos panels on a four-
ot unit grid was built in 1934 along the stream
Dow's father's garden.

rge windows to allow north light into the stu-
o are hinged at the top and closed by draw-
g them tightly against the jamb.

17

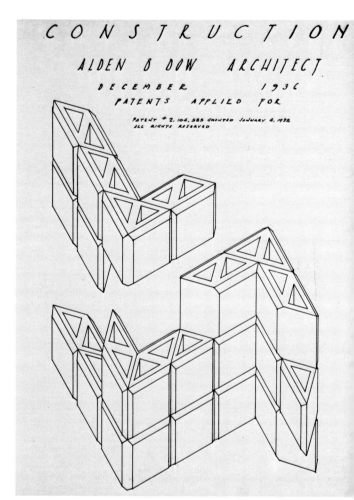

Dow designed these cinder concrete blocks, his Unit Blocks, in 1934 to create a wall of one-foot beveled squares that coordinate plan and elevation.

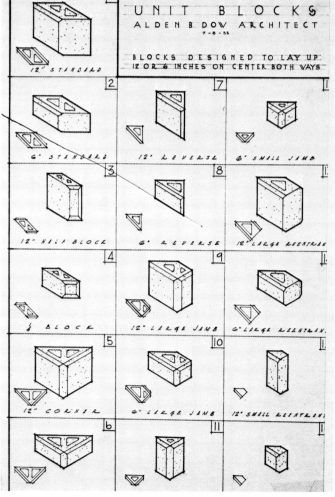

19

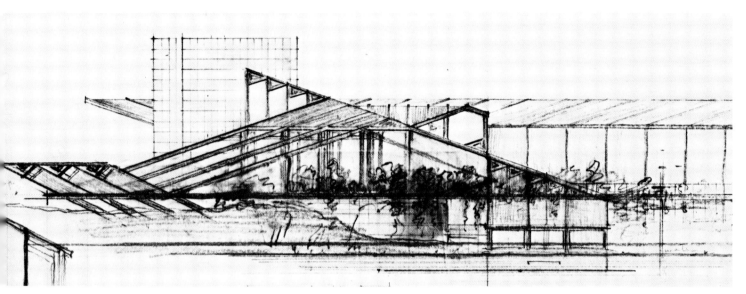

sketch of 1934–35 shows the studio conference room with its floor eighteen inches below
e waterline, terminating the long drafting room at the right. As built in 1935, large windows
d a floating, arrow-like roof replaced the closed conference room in the drawing, and a
ore elaborately constructed chimney replaced a single rectangular mass.

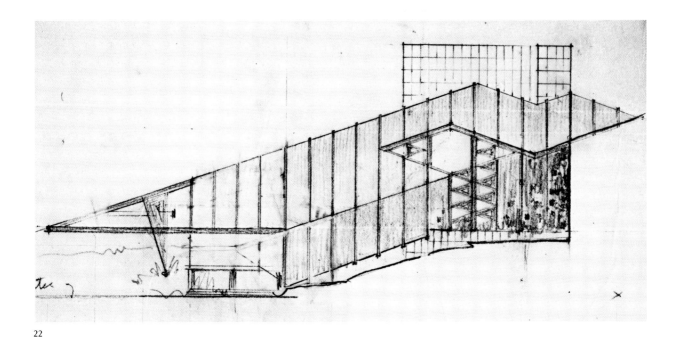

22

The exterior of the studio conference room is shown here at right angles to the view in Figures 20–21. The 4-in-12 roof slope is carried on toward the water at a 45-degree angle to the drafting room at the right.

23

The studio as it looked in 1937; to the right is the shop chimney at the end of a second studio wing. The integration of structure and landscape clearly demonstrates Dow's principle that "gardens never end and buildings never begin." 24

25

The building's orthogonal and diagonal patterns are extended far beyond the enclosed, habitable space. A trellis at the right prolongs the roof until it comes to rest on the scattered blocks or stepping stones.

3. Thinking about Architecture

Alden Dow's thoughts about architecture and matters of design in general were set forth in two talks that he gave in Midland in January, 1934, and April, 1935.[1] The first of these was given only months after he had returned from Taliesin, and we might expect considerable evidence of Wright's thought. However, the dominant idea of the first talk is a sensory stimulus theory that falls in the general category of the "picturesque." There are references to organic structure and the nature of materials in a discussion of materials as they are found in nature or are provided by human extraction and processing, but this follows a longer discussion of the nature of human beings, which focuses on the psychological effect of visual experience. Desirable visual effects on our senses and characters produce contentment, said Dow, and contentment balances extremes by the use of contrast.

Harmonizing the effects of contrast then becomes the architect's major task. Dow demonstrated the power of contrast in sensory stimulation by displaying the effects of color. Using colored gelatine transparencies and lengths of velvet, he showed how the red, blue, or green receptors in the eye can be sufficiently fatigued to seek relief in contrast. The compensating contrast of modern, rectangular lines in a table with a round bowl containing a natural arrangement of dark branches showed how line, another element of visual experience, obeys the same law of balance.

Dow's family tradition of the sciences also entered into this 1934 explanation as he proposed a common basis for art and science. Both organic structure and the psychology of perception stand on scientific principles. The principle of contrast was an important element in the study of perception made by, among others, William James. Dow had read Helmholtz's *Physiological Optics*, which includes a discussion of color and after-image. Dow proposed that, when employed scientifically, the results of contrast are "natural," but that contrast for contrast's sake is not natural. These effects are to be composed after the mechanical requirements of a house are satisfied.

In the second talk Dow reinforced the scientific basis of contrast by suggesting that "efficiency" is also derived from contrast. Human activity is a succession of movements and rests: "In applying these principles to a building, the aim is to produce a building with as many sources of nerve exercises as possible and at the same time the least amount of effort upon any one muscle." This sentence ties the argument to a venerable design tradition which includes Price and Knight. In his *Essays on the Picturesque* of 1794, Price recommended that smoothness and roughness should balance each other to avoid the danger of making these qualities too predominant. "If the whole building . . . were to be covered with sharp, projecting ornaments, the eye would be harassed and distracted and there would be a want of repose; on the other hand, if the whole were smooth and even, there would be a want of spirit and animation."[2]

The emphasis on balance is a very classical notion, and its presence in an aesthetic mode subsequently identified with Romantic agitation is a reminder of its origin in the eighteenth century. The highly irregular buildings of someone like Bruce Goff may seem examplars of the picturesque, but they lack the essential quality of repose that both the early proponents and later practitioners like Dow recommended. Dow's general approach to architectural design represents the survival of an aesthetic convention in a remarkably pure state. His loyalty to it is not a self-conscious choice so much as a continuation fostered by favorable social and economic circumstances.

Following this general principle of contrast, Dow in his second talk gives examples of the way it can be exercised. He begins with the convincing color demonstration which he had used so effectively the year before. Plain forms can be contrasted with angular or curved ones, especially when furniture, draperies, vases, or plants contrast with the usual architectural surfaces. Heavy-looking surfaces can be set against lighter grills or windows. Materials and texture can set up contrasts—wood paneling, masonry, and plaster. High rooms can be set against low and large against small. Lighting levels and even sound can be arranged to produce a natural balance of contrasts. Uvedale Price also extended his picturesque theory to include music, noting that discord can relieve the langor and weariness of continual smoothness but that imbalance of too much discord is to be avoided as well. A later exponent of progress through successive states of balance was Herbert Spencer (with whose thought Dow was familiar). In an 1852 essay he explained: "An essential prerequisite to all beauty is *contrast*. To obtain artistic effect light must be put in juxtaposition with shade, bright colors with dull colors, a fretted surface with a plain one. *Forte* passages in music must have *piano* passages to relieve them; concerted passages need interspersing with solos; and rich chords must not be continuously repeated."[3] A piece of music Dow admires very much, "Ein Heldenleben," by Richard Strauss, is a clear demonstration of this kind of thinking.

If the harmonizing of contrast is designed to achieve balance, Dow approaches architectural space with the intention of creating an unfolding continuity. Musical contrasts are sequential, not instantaneous, and movement through a building is its architectural equivalent. Dow recommends flowing visual connections between spaces, which, through a progression of compression and expansion, do not reveal everything at once. He says he learned this principle from his father's garden, where the spatial sequence was not obvious from a single viewpoint but constantly led one around some distant corner. For Uvedale Price this intricacy is achieved by "disposing objects which by a partial and uncertain concealment, excite and nourish curiosity."[4] This tradition was restated by the Arts and Crafts architect Barry Parker, who said in 1895, "There is great charm in a room broken up in plan where that slight feeling of mystery is given to it which arises when you cannot see the whole room from any one point in which you are likely to sit; when there is always something *round the corner*."[5] On this principle Dow uses half-levels, rooms opening onto other rooms through moveable wooden panels, and mirrors to create unfolding spaces inside his buildings.

The complication in Price's picturesque theory that troubled Richard Payne Knight and others was the relation of visual qualities to ideas. At its root, a sensory stimulus theory of aesthetics substitutes personal responses for a structure of intellectual concepts. The connections between objects of sight and ideas are rarely so direct as Price or Dow suggest. The effort to make such connections may arise from an uneasiness regarding the anti-intellectual bias of picturesque ideas. A sensory stimulus theory relies on the sensory apparatus of singular individuals. They may cultivate their responses, but they do not need to master an intellectual tradition of beauty. In his 1935 talk Dow included a brief outline of responses to visual conditions, citing intimacy, protection, privacy, and openness as feelings which must be combined in a balance of contrast. "Protection is brought about through walls and doors, while privacy is brought about through inconspicuousness, and intimacy is brought about through scale."

Colin Rowe has traced the compositional theory of design in an essay, "Character and Composition, Some Vicissitudes of Architectural Vocabulary in the Nineteenth Century."[6] The recurring problem for compositional theory was its ultimate waywardness. The task of writers and artists after Price was to apply a logical structure to sensory impressions. An antidote called "character" was applied by the High Victorians to the fitfulness of picturesque composition. Dow uses both character and structure as necessary controls on simple contrast. The ideal was Wright's "organic structure," based somehow on nature's lessons. The "unit system" geometry, the visual form of mathematics, supplied Dow with another control. Character was understood to be the expression of a building's purpose.

When the Midland Country Club building was opened in May, 1931, Dow was unable to attend because he was finishing his studies at Columbia. The *Midland Republican* asked him to supply some statement of his ideas and intentions. He wrote about the process by which logical design results in character and beauty. Employing a style rather than expressing character was illogical. An architect's task was to produce the right character or atmosphere for the social requirements of the project. The club had "a pleasing air and a very strong character which makes a perfect background for the development of personalities and characters,"[7] Dow told the newspaper, and went on to discuss the distinct and appropriate atmosphere for theaters, schools, hospitals, and houses.

In Rowe's argument, when style had been manipulated by the virtuosity of late Victorian architects like Richard Norman Shaw, further irrational elements complicated the organization of picturesque theory. As he observes, "By detaching the irrational element of style from the recently abstracted principles of composition, the dominant theory of the early twentieth century to some extent recapitulated at a more refined and sophisticated level the situation of c. 1830."[8] By 1930, the Columbia University School of Architecture was clearly part of this dominant theory of design. Although Rowe refers to books on composition from the early part of this century, they are not so clear in their presentation of balancing visual contrasts as are Dow or the theorists of a hundred years earlier.

As the son of a notably successful scientist, Dow sought to establish his chosen life's work on a foundation recognizable to scientists. Dow's father was somewhat reluctant to acknowledge architecture as an acceptable profession. He saw in it no chance for originality or objectivity. He himself could indulge his personal feelings as he laid out his garden or tended his orchids, but that was done "after hours." Dow worked hard to establish the connection between the two parts of his father's day. As far as he was concerned, "architecture is developing into a science in Midland. Psychology is entering into architecture," as what he called "mental comfort" becomes, for the first time, "one of the highest considerations in the new functional buildings."[9] The issues of psychology in architecture, the need for individual character in buildings, and the principles of contrast and harmony were much discussed when Dow was in school, as is evident in R. W. Sexton's 1929 publication *The Logic of Modern Architecture*.[10] For Dow, the man of science becomes the ideal client. He is not so concerned with appearing intellectual, nor is he lost in a romantic search for the good old days. Instead he is "full of life and ambition," and can approach the new architecture in the best frame of mind. (This hypothetical client was the archetype of the husbands of the women Dow was talking to at the time.)

A further guide to the Picturesque disposition of contrast was provided by making the composition understandable to the individual. Common sense should be satisfied by the contrasts as well as by the construction and materials. Dow has always been concerned with making his architecture accessible, with avoiding obscure forms that would require specialized training and wide cultural background to appreciate. "Architects must create a theory that the public can understand: in other words, a common language," as he put it in 1942.[11]

The conversational form of his thought is effective in face-to-face encounter, not in a lecture or a printed page. His conversational style is characterized by short segments on a single subject, almost like successive vignettes. In his *Architecture and Design*, published in 1943, photographs of his work are accompanied only by aphorisms like "architecture strives to stimulate the dwellers' interest; but the home is made by those who live in it" or "interest goes beyond the obvious."[12] Whenever he controlled the publication of his work, a similarly brief text takes the place of conventional captions.

In 1942 Dow began to compose his thoughts into diagrams that balance philosophical ideals, much as his architectural compositions contrast visual forms. In the *Pencil Points* article, a symmetrical diagram supports peace of mind as the goal of architecture. Equilibrium is reached by combining the forces of efficiency and comfort.[13] A diagram that appeared in his address to a symposium on creativity at Michigan State University in 1958 went far beyond the subject of the practice of architecture.[14] In this arrangement the human being is connected to divine affections by balancing individual rightness with social rightness in one's way of life. Individual rightness contains creativity, said Dow. It is "active, and love is its force." Social rightness contains laws; it is "passive; peace is its force."[15]

In Dow's latest expression of his thought, static balance is replaced by evolution, suggested by a circular form. The viewer is to supply the missing dimension of time to make the cycle a spiral. "A Way of Life Cycle" of 1976 is the most comprehensive statement of the ideas he has developed and depended upon for decades:

> The Way of Life Cycle starts with a person's individualism. In every way the individual is unique. The way I think is not exactly the way you do. Our unique abilities, when put together, naturally create something new. . . . this is called creativity. First you compose all the facts and all the feelings into an expression. The problem is to make that expression constructive, not destructive. To accomplish this you screen the expression for honesty, the give-and-take of humility, and the vitality of enthusiasm. Thus, expressions are developed. Evaluation and appreciation of these new expressions discourages the destructive and encourages the constructive. The results are ever finer standards of new expressions, thus we continue to travel around the Way of Life Cycle—forever improving, forever growing.

Dow's success with the single-family house grows naturally from his belief in the importance of the individual: "It seems to me that the destiny of architecture lies in . . . developing surroundings to promote the growth of individuals. Its importance is most obvious in the design of houses, for here the individual is supreme."[16] Dow's interest in Emerson and his admiration of Wright are two clear connections with the American tradition of individualism. A less familiar source appears in a letter to a client in which Dow mentions the Englishman Thomas Troward and his American follower Ernest S. Holmes.[17] These two admirers of Emerson are exponents of a nineteenth-century American "religion of healthy-mindedness" called New Thought, which mixed mental health with Emersonian philosophy. A major component of New Thought is the notion of a universal mind which overlaps each individual mind. The interaction of these two minds, one objective, the other subjective, is the source of creativity, but there is little emphasis on the interaction between the individual minds themselves. This isolation of the individual parallels the splintering effect which the Picturesque sensory aesthetic had on the shared ideals of classical taste.

As the son of a scientist-businessman, Dow tried in various ways, as we have seen, to ground his aesthetic ideals in the unifying concepts of science. In his Way of Life Cycle the unification of individuals is mentioned, but because neither the aesthetic nor the social ideals explicitly address the issue of generalized or anonymous social groups, Dow's designs for such groups lack the resolution of his houses or churches. The larger and more complex the building, the less direct an individual's identification with it and the less fully developed Dow's architectural response. Of course, a man prominent in nearly every group in his daily life may not be sympathetic to or familiar with anonymous settings. Dow has not needed to engage in anything so unseemly as argument to have his approach prevail. In his copy of Emerson's essays, he marked this sentence: "All just persons refuse to explain themselves and are content that new actions should do them that office."[18] For most people, even just ones who must argue a little to be heard, such a high ideal is a luxury.

Optimism about American progress based on free individual action comes naturally to successful people, and Dow has been closely associated for more than twenty years with an educational institution built on those principles. Northwood Institute has been his client and his publisher. Its philosophical foundation is that "the American competitive system educates for leadership in management and stresses productive attitudes and practices under the aegis of industry organizations." These organizations of the "free-enterprise elite" themselves create a free atmosphere, which is why "we have so much big industry, big business, mass production, mass prosperity and mass opportunity."[19]

For Dow, successful individuals are naturally pre-eminent, and challenges to their preferences or ideals are intrusions. An illustration of the paradox lying within his conception of individuality is his reaction to a display of variously sized colored cubes that was part of the Midland exhibit of his work in 1974. The cubes could be arranged as any visitor wished. When Dow went through the exhibit one afternoon, he adjusted a cube that someone had put on its edge rather than on its face, saying that the diagonal did not fit. A few years earlier, he noted that his father had removed a single magenta flower from a bed of red ones, remarking that it was uncharacteristic of this creative chemist not to make use of non-conforming elements to make something unexpected. Dow's own diagrams for his talk on creativity at Michigan State University had shown a diagonally placed block interrupting aligned ones. These anecdotes suggest that alterations in the composition are creative or offensive depending on who makes the changes.

The resolution of this difficulty flows naturally from Dow's aesthetic theory of sensory contrast. Whether interference is social or aesthetic, a balanced composition can be achieved if conflict is re-evaluated as contrast. Such a resolution is effective only if the intrusions take the form of variations within a framework of shared assumptions. Domestic design can be composed with this method, as can disagreements among friends. The composition of larger, more complex relationships is another matter that Dow has struggled with in thought and practice over the last fifty years.

By 1935 the aesthetic basis for his ideal of composition was in place. He had identified to his satisfaction the materials of compositional design and the guides to its use: comprehensibility, character, organic structure, and the laws of science. In 1945, his explanation of the design for the interiors of the Chemical Company sales office in St. Louis expanded the sensory stimulation and fatigue theory in this way:

Hold a weight in your hand and extend the arm out at a right angle to the body and hold it there for a few seconds. First your arm will become unbearably tired. Then your whole body experiences this fatigue. Finally drop your arm. If an easy chair is handy, you will slump down into it with the greatest of pleasure, for your entire body seems to crave rest even though you have used only a certain set of muscles in your arm. By overworking these muscles, you have apparently upset the equilibrium of your whole system. Recording of color with your eye has a similar effect.[20]

Herbert Spencer held a similar view of aesthetics: "Many elements of perception faculty must be called into play, while none are overexerted; there must be a great body of feeling arising from their moderate action, without the deduction of any pain from extreme action."[21] In 1948, in an address to the American Institute of Architects in Washington, Dow stated his view of composition in much the same terms he had used fourteen years before. In 1982 these principles are still the basis for "Composed Order," the latest formulation of his design thought.

So often architects' theory and practice are in conflict. Alden Dow is an architect who could control both factors more completely than most. When he exercised that control, his work is recognizably firmer than when he worked in less benign conditions. Although his design principles emphasize the visual effect of a building, Dow fully understood the necessity of solid construction and efficient planning and paid special attention to detail, both visual and constructional. There is no better demonstration of this than the well-sealed concrete "boat" that serves as the floor for the studio room which is sunk into the pond. Visual effect must be supported by mastery of construction—if Wright's roofs sometimes leaked, Dow's floor never has!

Notes

1. "Modern Architecture Makes Utility Beautiful, Says Dow," *Midland Republican*, January 25, 1934; "Dow Says Modern Architecture Is Common Sense Plus Sincerity," *Midland Republican*, April 25, 1935.

2. Price, *On the Picturesque*, p. 111.

3. Herbert Spencer, *Essays Scientific, Political and Speculative*, vol. 2 (New York, 1916), p. 373.

4. Price, *On the Picturesque*, p. 69.

5. Barry Parker and Raymond Unwin, "Of the Smaller Middle-Class House," *The Art of Building a Home* (London, 1901), p. 4.

6. *Oppositions 2*, January, 1974, pp. 41–60.

7. *Midland Republican*, April 30, 1931.

8. Rowe, "Character and Composition," p. 59.

9. Quoted in *Midland Republican*, May 18, 1937, p. 1.

10. *The Logic of Modern Architecture* (New York, 1929).

11. *Pencil Points*, May, 1942, p. 10.

12. *Architecture and Design*, June, 1943. This magazine was published in New York by the Architectural Catalog Company. The June issue was completely devoted to Dow's work.

13. *Pencil Points*, May, 1942, p. 275.

14. "An Architect's View of Creativity," in *Creativity and Its Cultivation*, edited by Harold H. Anderson (New York, 1959), pp. 30–43.

15. *Reflections* (Midland, 1970), p. 181.

16. "Planning the Contemporary House," *Architectural Record*, November, 1947, p. 90.

17. Letter to Fred Olsen, February 4, 1947.

18. Ralph Waldo Emerson, *Essays* (Boston, 1833), p. 75.

19. "The Northwood Idea," December 15, 1970, pp. 2, 4.

20. "The New St. Louis Blues," *Dow Diamond*, June, 1945, pp. 4–5.

21. Quoted in G. Baldwin Brown, *The Fine Arts* (New York, 1896), pp. 26–29.

4. Architectural Work before World War II

Alden Dow's architectural career can be divided in two at the year 1950. The predominant building type before this date was the private house. After 1950, a broader range of projects is represented, in work that is generally a simplification of his earlier style.

While at Taliesin, Dow was also beginning work on a small house. This second Midland house, on Main Street, was for Joseph A. Cavanagh, mayor of Midland from 1917 to 1920, a salesman for the Dow Chemical Company. On a standard lot which dropped off on the west to the river and railroad, Dow distributed carport, kitchen, and bedrooms in a line along the south boundary. At right angles to this alignment, the living room gained exposure to east and west (Figs. 26–27). The only roof overhang is at the carport and the entrance. Otherwise, like the Towsley house and the first plan for the Stein house, the shingled roof holds tightly to the mass of the building.

The drawings, organized on a four-foot unit system of grid lines used to lay out the plans, are beautiful small linen sheets with ink in five colors: brown for brick, yellow for wood framing, red for unit lines, blue for glass, and green for screening. The carpeting, plaster walls, edge-grain fir woodwork, and hot air heating make the interior a comfortable domestic environment (Fig. 28).

Dow initiated his interest in the design of low-cost houses with the F. W. Lewis house, the first sketches for which are dated 1933 but which was built in 1934 for $2,500. Lewis was an accountant for the Dow Chemical Company. Two bedrooms, living room, built-in dining table, and kitchen are compactly arranged on a four-foot unit system within a twenty-eight-foot-square plan (Fig. 29). The exterior is very simply clad with masonite attached to the wooden frame by battens. Windows are simple, four-by-four-foot or four-by-two-foot top-hinged sash (Fig. 30). The roof slopes are brought together at the central chimney and covered inside with Celotex divided by wood battens. A slight spatial variety is introduced by lowering the living and kitchen half of the house; they are one step down from the entrance, bedrooms, and bath (Fig. 31). The plans are presented in a red poché.

The central chimney of the Lewis house is one of the early appearances of the Unit Block Dow developed. The first project using the blocks throughout was the house for Mr. and Mrs. Lynn Heatley, the drawings for which are dated 1933. The red poché plan is regulated by a four-foot unit system. The twenty-eight-foot width and centrally located chimney recall the Lewis house, but the four bedrooms, which extend the length to sixty-eight feet, the flat roof, and the attached garage make it a much different house (Fig. 32). Variation in the vertical dimension is accomplished by three roof levels: the lowest at the garage, entrance and half the kitchen; the main roof over the remainder of the house; and a clerestory over the entrance hall, a corner of the dining room, and the living room at the chimney. The floor is on three levels as well: lowest in the middle of the house, up a foot to the living room at the front, and up two feet to the bedrooms and bath at the back. Continuity from inside to outside is produced by a Unit Block floor entering the house at the front door and continuing up to the living room hearth and to the raised bedroom hall and the back terrace. Horizontal roof planes at several levels intersect the four-foot-square block chimney (Fig. 33).

The Heatley house was not built. The first Unit Block house to be built was the Sheldon B. Heath house, which Dow designed in the first half of 1934. An explanatory note in the specifications introduced the contractors to the layout of the drawings:

> The elimination of many dimensions on these drawings has been accomplished by the adoption of a unit system. Units being indicated on plans by faint lines forming four-foot squares, and on elevations by vertical lines four feet apart. All dimensions are figured to these unit lines and all details refer to them. The virtue of the system lies in the elimination of arbitrary figured dimensions and the ease with which work can be checked. Considerable expedition in building and freedom from mistakes will result from a grasp of its essentials.

A departure from traditional materials is noted in the section of the specifications on masonry work: "Certain walls in this house as indicated are to be of a new style of cinder concrete block which has been developed in the architect's office. It is a block that offers many new features in construction and design and so far has met with considerable enthusiasm. This will be the first building of importance to use it and because of its many new features which are all strange to the contractor, the blocks, mortar and labor for placing them will not enter into this contract."

This four-bedroom house on a flat site was one of the first to be located in a new residential development near the Midland Country Club. A chemist at the chemical company, Heath was willing that his own house be as experimental as his work at the plant. Its appearance, from the street, is striking: an extended horizontal roof topped by a clerestory and a chimney enclosing a skylight (Fig. 34).

For Alden Dow this house represented a major step forward in his residential designs. The sunken garden exposing the lower rooms had been used in the first two houses Dow built in Midland, but the blocks and the flat roof introduced elements that he composed in varying arrangements for the next seven years or so until he abandoned the Unit Blocks. The front elevation is extended by trellises cantilevered four to eight feet by means of steel beams and channels. But the house is in fact longer from front to back. The rear bedroom-dining room portion is clean, compact, and contained rather than dramatically extended (Fig. 35).

The dominant feature of the major rooms is the elaborate fireplace-chimney-skylight that serves as the focus for living room, library, and dining room. The chimney mass rises in two piers above the clerestory, whose glass is continued at a slant to fill in the gap between the two piers (Fig. 36). The light pouring in at a point which is solid and dark in most houses is striking. The detail and ornamental expression of wood structure makes this house a richly composed textural artifact. The lower ceilings are plastered; the high ceilings are articulated by rafters on two-foot centers which are exposed in the kitchen and enclosed in the bedrooms, the dining room, and the library, where they turn upward into the skylight. Between these rafters, all running parallel with the front elevation, are two-foot-square plywood panels with alternating directions of the grain. The pattern of the Unit Block walls is varied by scattered small glass panes and quarter-sized blocks set off by stucco panels and areas of mullioned windows in broad panels or bands. The play of high, textured ceilings against lower plaster ones, the contrast of dominant light buff with blue and red accents—all demonstrate Alden Dow's compositional interests at an early stage. At the same time, the plan is effectively zoned for functional convenience. Features like a pass-through window from kitchen to dining room make this a most serviceable house.

In 1934, within three blocks of the Heath house, Dow designed two other Unit Block houses, for Alden W. Hanson and John S. Whitman. The Hanson house, for Alden Dow's brother-in-law, a physicist at Dow Chemical, is a compact, three-bedroom structure, planned to be enlarged according to a three-foot unit system. As Dow described the house in *Architectural Forum* several years later, "the plan provides low cubage for kitchen, dining room and lower bedroom which are located below grade and rest on the earth. This arrangement is economical, makes for cooler rooms in summer and provides an interesting view of the planting outside."[1] The almost symmetrical initial plan was weighted in favor of the entrance side by a large Unit Block chimney mass, which produces an inglenook at the hearth in the high-ceilinged living room on the half level between the kitchen-dining area below and the bedrooms above (Figs. 37–39).

The John S. Whitman house achieved fame far beyond its home town of nine thousand. It won the grand prize for residential architecture at the 1937 Paris Exposition of Arts and Technology. The house's relatively simple exterior of continuous, horizontal layering encloses an interior on five levels, stepping up and around a stair (Fig. 40). The spatial arrangement fits together so effectively that what may seem like a puzzle in the abstract makes immediate sense in the carefully zoned living arrangement. The three bedrooms are at the top level over the entrance and garage. At the lowest level is the game room, five steps below the entrance. Between these lie kitchen and dining room on one level and living room on another (Fig. 41). As in the Heath house, the clerestory over the hearth in the living room continues as bedroom windows once it passes the chimney mass (Fig. 42).

John Whitman was from an old Midland family. His grandfather, the first "white man" in the area, came to the county from Vermont in 1836. His father was a security employee of the chemical works. John Whitman had worked with Alden Dow's father when he was mayor from 1921 to 1930. During that period he also served as chairman of the building committee for the Midland County Courthouse. His businesses included coal, ice, and sand. In 1925 he began manufacturing cinder blocks. Of course his own house was constructed of Dow's Unit Blocks made in his own yard.

The interior of the house is a carefully assembled composition of low and high, open and closed. The woodwork inside and out is Louisiana red cypress (Fig. 43). Dow's interest in the colors of the house as well as its volumes, masses, and textures is evident in the bathrooms. In the owner's bath, his specifications called for the walls to be peach and the fixtures green; in the hall bath the walls were tan and the fixtures lavender. Carpeting throughout dining and living areas was turquoise and draperies were red with blue. The built-in seat by the living room hearth was covered by striped material combining all the colors of the room, including the blue hearth tile. In the interest of textural and color continuity, fire brick was not used in the living room or game room fireplaces; as a result, they were rarely used.

After working with Unit Blocks in these three houses to produce visually satisfying patterns and coordinated relations between coursing and window and door openings, Dow found the tight discipline required by the blocks restrictive. The occasional frame and plaster wall must have seemed as much a relief to the designer as it was to the viewer's eyes.

Interest in housing in Midland was not only stimulated by Alden Dow's five distinctive examples. In the mid-thirties Midland was more receptive than other cities to such encouragement because of the full employment provided at the chemical plant and the national concern for adequate housing as a social need as well as a stimulus to the economy. In 1934 the weekly *Midland Republican* sponsored the construction of an "educational home" by developers from Jackson, Michigan, Mr. and Mrs. Victor Nurmi. The front-page coverage given the Nurmis' "modified colonial" house brought the backward stylistic approach that Dow was resisting mightily right into his own territory.[2] Nor did his connection with the chemical company guarantee acceptance of his new houses: Mr. and Mrs. A. W. Beshgatoor, fellow members of the Midland Country Club, built a "French modern" provincial house in 1936 in the same neighborhood as the Heaths, Hansons, and Whitmans.

In the next seven years, up to the outbreak of World War II and his association with the Dow Chemical Company developments in Texas, Dow explored variations on two house types, the sloped-roof brick model and the flat-roofed Unit Block model. Occasionally he experimented in the early design stages of smaller houses with both roof forms. His few non-residential commissions were nearly all for Dow Chemical.

Dr. Charles MacCallum came to Dow in 1935 to design a house on his lot to the north of the country club. In the spring Dow made several studies for the sloping property, using his Unit Blocks. The first scheme arranged the rooms in a line along the crest of the hill. From the entrance one saw a low, one-story house with a hipped roof. From the downhill side, the house's two stories were fully exposed. The block walls were disposed as free-standing screens and enclosing angles, separated by windows emphasized by continuous mullions between the two floors.

In May, Dow had developed a second Unit Block plan for MacCallum in an L-shape on a four-foot unit system. Except for the playroom below and a crow's-nest study overlooking the living room above the entrance, the house was on one level. The final plan, drawn in December, is much freer and more asymmetrical (Fig. 44). This luxurious house was finally constructed of brick, like the Stein house, rather than block, in part because of family connections with a brick supplier (Figs. 45–46). The ornamental detail of the living room is beautifully drawn in ink on linen sheets, organized on an eight-foot unit system. At the living room and playroom windows cypress trim encloses small panes of red glass (Figs. 47–48). This garden facade is rich in colors and textures, with wide plaster soffits spreading along the brick piers and retaining walls, wood window frames, copper sheathing, and clear and red glass. Dow again used Acoustex squares in this house for the ceiling and for one wall of the playroom beneath the living room.

Another brick pitched-roof house designed during 1935 was for Oscar C. Diehl, two blocks from the Steins. This two-bedroom house recalls both the MacCallum and Cavanagh houses, but on a flat site (Fig. 49). In addition to the brick and copper, a distinctive texture is introduced by the diamond-leaded glass in the living room (Fig. 50). Both cypress and birch are used in the interior of this small house (Fig. 51). The balanced contrast of color is present in the dressing room, with green carpet and red upholstery on the stool. This small corner of the bedroom is enlivened by a large mirror that reflects hidden lamps above it and is lighted at floor level by a frosted glass sill.

Howard Ball of the sales department at Dow Chemical Company got a simpler Unit Block house up the street from the Hansons and the Heaths. Like them, it is laid out on a four-foot unit system and achieves spatial variation by locating the living room at mid-level between dining room, kitchen, and maid's rooms below and two bedrooms above the dining room and kitchen. In 1938 the kitchen was expanded and a study on the lower level and a bedroom above it were added. This house, which was built at about half the cost of the Diehl house, used clear fir carpentry both inside and out, but the textural contrasts of block, plaster, and window groups integrated the composition.

Frank Lloyd Wright's development of the Usonian house at Taliesin during 1934 and 1935 makes an intriguing parallel with Dow's work in Midland during these same years.[3] The two projects Dow presented in July, 1935, to Margaret Mitts are masterful expressions of open, expansive residences for informal, modern living. (Unfortunately, Miss Mitts did not pursue her building plans after seeing Dow's presentation drawings.) Although these two houses are flat-roofed Unit Block examples, they are extended freely in a linear fashion in response to their cramped location along the property lines of Miss Mitts' large lot, which was already occupied by an older house. The first house (Figs. 52–53) is the simpler of the two; it has only two bedrooms raised half a level behind a large chimney mass. The second house (Figs. 54–55) is a larger residence of three bedrooms. The half-level variation here is used to elevate a master bedroom suite with fireplace over the kitchen and dining room. The living room is open on two sides to a sunken garden framed by a low block wall.

It is not clear what communication between Midland and Taliesin was taking place during this time, but Dow's opportunities to build several open-plan small houses may have interested Wright. The most marked difference between, say, his projects for Miss Mitts and Wright's Hoult (1935) and Lusk (1935–36) projects and the first Jacobs house (1936) is in the degree of finish: Wright's Usonian model could, and did, become opulent in later years, but the initial formulation was unmistakably spartan.

The first of Dow's many commercial projects for the Dow Chemical Company was the 1935 remodeling and addition to its main office building. Two existing buildings were linked in a composition of brick masses sheltering a glass entrance (Fig. 56). The new entrance was opened in January, 1936. Among other work done for the chemical company is a patent records and library stack and storage project of 1937, a composition of brick masses edged with narrow window bands in the style of the Dutchman Willem Dudok.

The grandest commission that Dow was given at this period came from the newly elected board chairman of the Dow Chemical Company, James T. Pardee, and his wife, Elsa. Pardee had been in Dow's father's class at the Case School of Applied Science in Cleveland. The Pardees maintained a home in Cleveland for the winter months and spent summers in Midland. They approached Dow at the end of 1935 with a request for a new house to replace one on Main Street across from the Stein house. During construction of their new house they stayed in Cleveland. By the end of January, Dow had preliminary plans ready and sent them off.

In the ensuing three months various adjustments were made by architect and client (Fig. 57). Two major issues needed to be resolved: the question of whether the construction material would be brick or cinder block and of whether the house had too many windows or not enough. Brick was recognized as appropriate for a formal residence; cinder block was not. Mrs. Pardee, whose role as board chairman's wife included extensive social activities, was not entirely delighted by the idea of a house made of Dow's Unit Blocks, nor were friends in Cleveland, though Mrs. Pardee was careful to say to their engineer husbands that she herself liked cinder block. Dow sent her a colored pencil perspective of a Unit Block house, which Mrs. Pardee found "very pretty. If you can make a more pleasing house of cinder block, I can change my mind."[4] Dow accompanied his sketches with a letter explaining his preference for the block. He had tried working with brick veneer, as in the Stein house, he wrote, but "the effects gained by using cinder block like the Heaths' house make it seem a great mistake not to use them. They have a much quieter feeling and create a continuity that is very difficult to get with the bricks because the bricks do not work into any geometric pattern conforming with window openings and the like."[5]

The matter of windows still concerned Mrs. Pardee three years after moving in, when she complained that she could not entertain on bright days. There had always been too much glass for her taste in Dow's designs. During the planning stages she asked whether one of the windows toward Main Street could not be removed. Dow replied: "Although in the plans it may appear like a lot of window space in the living room, I am sure that this is not excessive and is one of the features of the house. To cut down this would mean upsetting the whole scheme of this room and the elevation of the house."[6] The second-level bedrooms facing the park were glazed along their entire length. Mrs. Pardee did not need so many windows and wondered whether some wall surface might be introduced for privacy, with the understanding that such an alteration should not adversely affect the looks of the house.

In June, 1936, the construction contract for the house was signed. The drawings for this $50,000 house are remarkable. One hundred and fifty sheets, of which ninety-four are full-size details, describe minutely how it was to be fitted together. The plans, elevations and sections are beautifully drawn on linen in black ink highlighted with brown, blue, red, and green. The structural steel is presented in an axonometric drawing. The top of the T-shaped plan faces northwest to the park across the street. The house is ninety feet long; it begins at the corner of Main Street with the living room, then there is a game room, and at the end a garage entered from the rear. Above the game room and garage are the guest bedroom and master suite. The entrance is along the stem of the T, which contains maids rooms and kitchen (Fig. 58). The dining room fills the northeast juncture of the T (Fig. 59).

Altogether, the Pardee house is a simple one made exceptional by its elaboration. The rooms are generous in size; for example, the master bedroom-dressing room suite is twenty-five by thirty feet. Drawers for the extensive case work in the house are all on roller bearings. The house was fully air-conditioned and steam-heated. Kitchen equipment included a dishwasher. The interior woodwork is straight edge-grain Louisiana red cypress. The beds and the pearwood dining room table, which were designed by Dow, were made by Bonhard Art Furniture in Cleveland.

All of these specialty items took their places in a cinderblock house trimmed in copper. The Midland paper published a photograph of the house at the end of June, 1937, and the Pardees moved in shortly after. It was also featured in an article on Dow's houses in Midland in *Life*.[7] In 1953 Carl Gerstaker added a second floor with two bedrooms over the enlarged service wing.

In Saginaw, Dow designed a house on a narrow town lot for his aunt, Mary Dow. The site was next to a church and required some ingenuity in providing privacy for this three-bedroom house of Unit Block and glass block, copper and cypress (Fig. 60). The major drawings of February, 1936, are organized by the four-foot unit system on eleven small sheets. The remainder of the thirty-eight sheets are larger presentations of details. Dow raised the living room half a level above the street-front garage and the rear part of the house, which contains kitchen, dining room, and one bedroom

49

(Figs. 61–62). The front door, four by seven feet, is a generous welcome to the living room with its two ceiling heights, low at the windows, high at the fireplace. Two bedrooms overlook the living room through hinged wooden panels. Dow's interest in the forms, textures, and colors of plant materials is manifested in the planting list from the Bay City Nursery. Evergreens included Austrian and Mugho pines, juniper, blue spruce and yews, and euonymus. Deciduous plants included birch, Japanese maple, weeping willow, and Russian olive. Lilacs, honeysuckle, mock orange, crab apples, plum, viburnum, roses, delphinium, hollyhocks, tulips, hyacinths, and iris provided color. Mary Dow clearly loved plants, but the architect's concern for the composition of building and vegetation is also evident in his studio and the renderings of his houses, particularly the two projects for Margaret Mitts.

Dow designed two examples of the pitched-roof residence in 1936 as well. The first was next door to the MacCallums, for George Greene, who worked for Dow Chemical. Even though the Greene house uses brick rather than the Unit Blocks, it is drawn with a four-foot unit system. Along with the Saunders house, designed in the same period, it shows Dow's exploration of angled elements in his house plans. Here Greene's living and dining rooms are turned at 45 degrees (Figs. 63–65). A red-green color scheme is again present in the green carpet and pink brick.

The second sloped-roof scheme of 1936 is in Bloomfield Hills, around the corner from Cranbrook Academy. S. Gordon Saunders, who worked for the Dodge division of Chrysler Corporation, had a lot on a small retaining pond which suggested Dow's studio site (Fig. 66). The drawings are organized by four-foot units, with seven main sheets and eighty-nine sheets of details. The living room is the lowest level, one foot below the water line. The submerged floor is similar to Dow's studio conference room: two concrete shells more than a foot thick are separated by five plys of felt membranes. In this house and others the larger open space required pipe columns in framed walls to support standard steel beams. In contrast to the Greene house, the Saunders house plan contains several complex angled walls at both ends (Fig. 67). The varying levels and angular relationships result in an interesting folding and cutting of a basically simple hipped roof. In November, 1937, Saunders wrote to Dow reporting that he had been up to see his Charles Bachman house in Lansing (Bachman was the Michigan State football coach) and thought it was "a knockout."

The Koerting house in Elkhart, Indiana, is a similar example of the cubic, flat-roofed residence, though the Bachman house includes some Unit Block, while the Koerting house uses only plaster. They are both organized on a four-foot unit system with the dominant surfaces plaster on frame, but the materials in the Koerting house are more substantial. There is a copper cornice, cypress is used on the exterior, and maple and birch inside. Because the Bachman house is set into a low bank, the main living areas, including three bedrooms, are all on the second level, reached by an open stair behind the chimney mass (Fig. 68).

Planting plans for both houses are given. For Bachman the slopes next to the dining room are to be heavily planted in birch, pine, juniper, euonymus, hollyhock, and delphinium. At the living room slope are pine, mugho pine, blue spruce, juniper, sumac, and shad bush. The Koerting house is located on the north bank of the St. Joseph River. Its planting plan included pine, willow, Russian olive, plum, juniper, and sumac.

William E. Koerting worked for Miles Laboratories, which did business with Dow Chemical. His father was a United States consul in Tokyo, and shortly after the house was finished the elder Koertings arrived with three cases of Japanese curios, which Dow's design displayed to advantage. The Dows and the Koertings developed a congenial relationship during and after construction. When Dow took a special personal interest in the client, he would provide a vivid narrative with the plans. A letter to Mr. Koerting describes a tour through the house that relates to the client what the architect was seeing in his mind's eye (Figs. 69–70):

> As you note, there are three levels. The reason for this is that the water level of the river seems a bit too high to get an ordinary height basement under the house without raising the grade considerably. In order to get away from such a low basement, I have raised the living room floor half a story and put the basement under this particular area only. The garage is placed in the front and as shown because it seems to be the easiest way to operate the car. The garage is connected with the house by a wide over-hanging roof which allows protection for landing and also protects both the main entrance and service entrance.

After some explanation of floor plan and discussion of positions of entrances, terraces, and porch, Dow continues:

> The wall separating this bedroom from the living room I have indicated [to be] of wood paneling with swinging panels opening out into the living room at the height of the rail of the balcony. This would produce a very interesting effect from below and in the bedroom, and it would tend to tie these two rooms together. Outside of these doors, on the living room side, there would be a wide shelf or deck, as shown, which would tie into the balcony railing. This shelf should offer a chance for some interesting effects as a place for ferns or other pieces of ornaments. The deck along the opposite side of the living room would furnish similar possibilities. You will note that the plans are laid out on a system of squares. These units are four feet square and will assist you in determining the size of the various rooms. Just count the number of squares.[8]

51

The variation in room height in this well-built house is an expression of the principle of contrast. It caused Mr. Koerting some concern because some ceilings and windows were very low. The interior color scheme was very simple: cherry red carpeting throughout the main floor, off-white walls, and white draperies. Mrs. Koerting's grand piano stood below the bedroom balcony in front of a large Japanese screen. In July of 1937, Mr. Koerting was "digging up enough capital" to build, and ran into a familiar case of reluctance to lend for "modern" architecture on the part of the FHA.[9]

The legal status of such a modern building was explicitly determined in the Millard Pryor house, designed early in 1937 by Dow for a new subdivision in Grosse Pointe Park, east of Detroit. A Circuit Court opinion by Judge Homer Ferguson was rendered on May 4, 1938, on the suit brought by the Windmill Point Land Commission against Mr. Pryor for non-compliance with its building restrictions. The issue was a trellis, supported by a pier, which projected from the front of the house and ended twenty-four feet from the sidewalk (Fig. 71). When Dow was called upon to testify in the case, he said that the architect has to "satisfy not only the physical being of the building and owner, but he has to satisfy the mental being of the builder and owner." Judge Ferguson stated in his opinion: "Mr. Dow explains that he had a rather 'blocky' house, a small house; he had some 150 feet; he had to make it appear as if it was growing out of the entire lot instead of merely being on the lot. To do that he erected what he says is a porch some 36 or 38 feet long. The pier objected to is to support the top structure. I am satisfied that modern architecture has erected this part of the building as a porch. It helps to place the house in a pleasant surrounding."[10]

A further complaint was the insufficiency of the stucco surface on the cinder block (not Dow's Unit Blocks). The judge ruled that stucco "has been used on this building, even though it was put on with a blow machine."[11]

Mrs. Pryor reassured Dow just before the hearing that the house really looked lovely.[12] Millard and Mary Pryor had been introduced to Dow by letter in December of 1936. Pryor wrote to Dow in February that he was "very much interested in your work, having seen, from the outside, several of the houses you built in Midland."[13] The Pryors' requirements for a family that included twin boys and a maid were supplied: bedrooms for parents, boys, guest, and maid; two baths; two-car attached garage; cost not over $15,000 ($3,000 for the lot, $12,000 for the house and furnishings).

By April 27, 1937, Dow had worked up two similar schemes, only the smaller of which was developed to completion (Fig. 72). Dow used the architectural firm of G. M. Merritt and Lyle S. Cole as Detroit consultants for the job. The materials of the house are simple: clear fir, glass block, and standard eight-by-eight-by-sixteen-inch cinder blocks. Its European starkness is striking. The spatial subtlety of the Pryor house is confined to the single-level shaft of space with the entrance at one end and the notorious trellis-pier at the other. The proposed color scheme for the house appears in Dow's letter to Millard Pryor:

If you use a brown carpet, the fireplace seat should be covered in purple, blue, blue-green, or green color. Whichever one you pick for this will more or less determine the other colors to be used. . . . Over this seat you should have a half-dozen pillows varying in size from twelve inches square up to two feet square. These I believe would be well in yellow, red, and white. The remaining chairs in the living room ought to be done in grass green and bright blue, and all other little trinkets around the room ought to run toward red.

The two-story glass block wall in the living room immediately caused the Pryors concern because of its uncontrolled glare (Fig. 73). Dow had used glass block in the MacCallum and Mitts houses, but always in protected locations. Pryor wondered whether a thin coat of paint might reduce the glare. Instead, Dow suggested an awning arrangement of two-foot-wide strips of white canvas, spaced two inches apart, stretched from the roof to a pipe eight feet above the ground. This shading device was to fill in for a willow tree until it grew sufficiently. The importance of the tree was underscored when Dow purchased it for the site after the Pryors said that they could not do so, as they had already exceeded their budget.

In the fall of 1938 Mrs. Pryor wrote to Dow about their adventure with modern architecture after the success of their court case: "The more we live in our house, the better we like it, and even those of our friends who started out to feel sorry for us are coming around to the realization that there's nothing like a modern house for really living. Such comments as we've had. A maid who came for an interview asked me if this were a funeral parlor. I just loved that. An amazing number of people have come in to rave and ask questions."[14]

Dow's response to the technologies being used and developed at the chemical plant was to find ways to apply them to architectural purposes. In the late thirties, Dow Chemical was working with plastics, and he developed a plastic sheet equivalent to his Unit Blocks. These unit sheets, 11¾ inches square, were to be attached to walls framed with 12-inch-on-center studs. Three alternatives for fastening them are shown in a drawing of July, 1937. Various flange and clip alternatives were used to attach the sheets to the two-by-four-inch frame. The joints over the studs were to be caulked. In the same month, the unit sheets appeared in the design for a most unusual house in the form of a twenty-five-foot cube. The colored pencil perspective of the project, entitled "1940" (Fig. 74), shows a singular orange block covered by a one-foot-square grid. Examples of projects which would use the square plastic sheets appeared in the Dow Company magazine and in an *Architectural Record* article on plastic in July, 1940. There, models are shown which look rather like the Mitts' houses. The sheets were actually included in only two buildings: a two-story stair tower in the Dow Chemical Main Office Building and along the fascia and soffit of a bathhouse in Midland. The

Dow Chemical exhibit at the 1939 Golden Gate Exposition in San Francisco was also based on the square sheets of Ethocel and Styron which Alden Dow used as display cases for various products (Fig. 75). The Koertings reported to Dow that they saw the exhibit: "Both Helen and myself immediately recognized the man who built it. It is simply beautiful."[15]

The K. T. Keller project of 1938–40 and the Anderson Arbury house of 1939 are two of the grandest Unit Block houses Dow was to design. Beginning in the spring of 1938, the Kellers got a series of plans and perspectives from Dow. Hillhouse was a Unit Block and copper-roof complex of two houses stretching for 256 feet along the top of a hill overlooking Lake St. Clair. Its luxurious plan, one room deep, organized on a four-foot unit, had three servants' bedrooms, a large kitchen, and a thirty-foot-long dining room on the lower level. Three bedrooms and a living room were at entrance level (Fig. 76). The Garden House was a smaller, two-story brick house with flat roofs on several levels; it looked something like the Pryor house. In December of 1938 a diagonal was introduced into the Hill House plan which brought the linear house into a somewhat more compact arrangement. The last proposal to Keller in February, 1940, was a linear plan only eighty-four feet long, with the garage perpendicular to the house and connected to it by a pergola.

Gordon Saunders had brought together Dow and Keller, the man who succeeded Walter Chrysler as chief executive officer of the Chrysler Corporation in 1940. Their discussions in Midland early in 1938 about body design whetted Dow's interest in tackling this new design problem. He wrote to Saunders: "I just have a feeling that the next Chrysler body design is going to come out of this office." He hoped to "get hold of one of those skeleton chassis models on which they build plaster models and keep it . . . for a couple of months."[16] (Dow owned a Chrysler Airflow and later bought his brother's Scarab.) For one reason or another, this foray into automotive design did not go further.

Anderson Arbury was Dow's brother-in-law. His house had burned down in January of 1935. In 1939 Dow designed a Unit Block house for him on an unprecedented scale and at an unprecedented cost. The three-by-five-foot drawings are in ink on linen. The house, which looks strangely undomestic (Fig. 77), is organized in pinwheel fashion, with the center on the entrance at the intersection of four wings and the chimney of the sunken living room (Fig. 78). One of the four wings contains bedrooms; the opposite wing contains a kitchen and dining room (Fig. 79). Each of these terminates with a forty-five-degree shift of the rectilinear grid (Fig. 80). The other two wings are the twenty-four-foot-square living room, with a quarter-circle of built-in seating around the fireplace, and a three-car garage at the end of an eighty-foot covered walkway.

In the same year, Dow designed an extended Unit Block house for A. W. Hodgkiss, a road-builder in Petoskey. Overlooking Lake Michigan, the three-bedroom house is more than a hundred feet long with garage and terrace (Fig. 81). The owner kept costs down by himself providing the labor and materials for the masonry and carpentry. Aside from the blocks, the Hodgkiss house is a simpler arrangement of volumes and textures, indicating the trend of Dow's subsequent work.

After the Keller project and the Arbury house, there were only three more Unit Block houses built. Dow's own house, which was designed in 1939, will be described in the last chapter. The LeRoy Smith house in Algonac of 1940 and the Robbie Robinson house of 1941 were built using the blocks. The Smith house, located on the St. Clair River, is a squarish house with a living room and two bedrooms on the second floor. Robbie Robinson, the Hope's Window representative in Detroit, had worked with Dow since the Stein house. The Unit Block in this squarish house is used primarily around the living room and second floor bedrooms on the front. The remainder of the house is stucco on frame.

After the war, the Unit Block concrete forms were taken to Florida by a fast-talking developer connected with the railroad unions. That nothing ever came of his grand housing plans came as no surprise to some of Dow's staff. The disappearance of their textural pattern and planning discipline removed an important element in Dow's architectural palette.

Notes

1. *Architectural Forum*, April, 1937, p. 354.

2. *Midland Republican*, October 18, 1934, p. 1.

3. See John Sergeant, *Frank Lloyd Wright's Usonian Houses*, Whitney Library of Design (New York, 1976).

4. Mrs. James Pardee to Dow, February 25, 1936.

5. Dow to Mrs. James Pardee, February 21, 1936.

6. Dow to Mrs. James Pardee, March 16, 1936.

7. "Midland, Michigan, Leads Way in Private Housing," *Life*, November 15, 1936, p. 50.

8. Dow to William Koerting, February 5, 1937.

9. William Koerting to Dow, July 19, 1937.

10. *Windmill Point Land Company* v. *Millard Pryor*, Circuit Court of Wayne County, Michigan, filed February 25, 1938, Judge Homer Ferguson opinion of May 4, 1938.

11. *Ibid.*

12. Mrs. Millard Pryor to Dow, April 16, 1938.

13. Millard Pryor to Dow, February 2, 1937.

14. Letter of Autumn, 1938.

15. Letter of August 4, 1939.

16. Letter of February 17, 1938.

Architectural Work before World War II / ILLUSTRATIONS

26

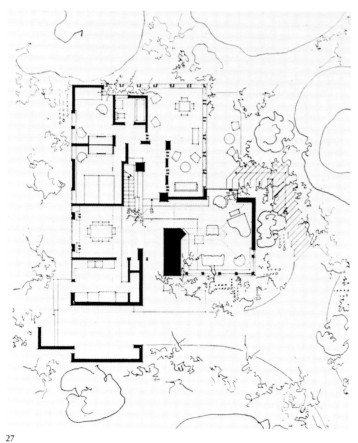

27

Joseph A. Cavanagh house, Midland, 1933–34. This house is similar to t[?] Stein house in arrangement. The lower level bedrooms and the sitting roo[?] are exposed at the back by the sloping site. The house is a composition [?] balanced contrasts: sloped and flat ceilings, plaster and brick-and-woo[?] shelves, and dining room windows in the back.

28

31

W. Lewis house, Midland, 1933–34. Its square com-
pactness is the result of Dow's investigation of the
low-cost house. Its wood and masonite construction
system was also used in the first stage of Dow's
studio. The slope of the roof is exposed in the front
room and in the bedrooms at the back (Fig. 31).
Through the middle third of the house a flat deck
lowers the height of the entrance, hall, and bathroom. Unit Blocks are used in the hearth and
chimney.

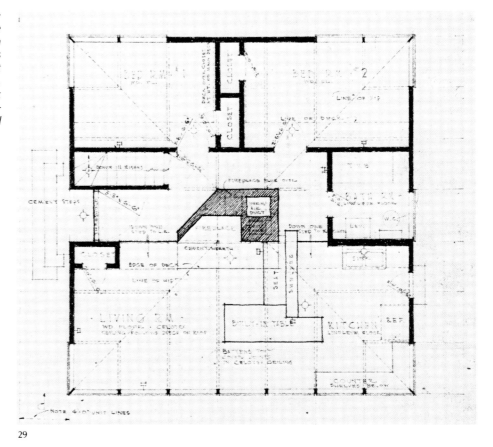

29

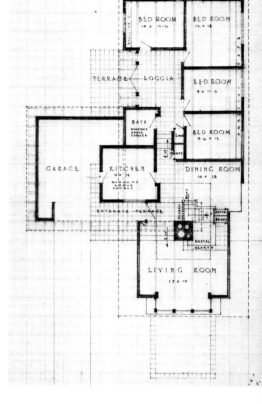

Project for Lynn Heatley house, Midland, 1933. For the first time Dow used the Unit Blocks for a complete house. Within a compact volume, the house is varied through different floor and ceiling levels. An extension beyond the unpunctured Unit Block walls is implied by the glass corner window in the dining room and the overhang of the thin roof lid beyond the living room windows (Fig. 33).

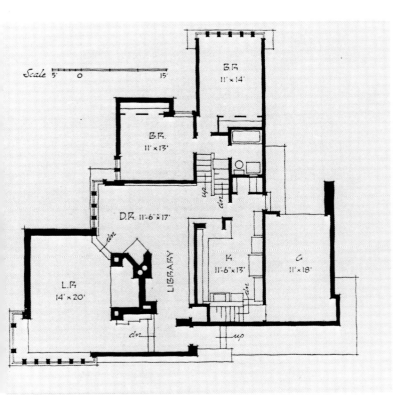

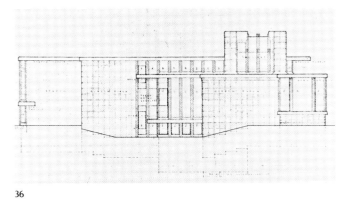

36

Sheldon B. Heath house, Midland, 1934. The front elevation (Fig. 34) differentiates the rooms behind it — living room, entrance, kitchen, and garage — while it unifies them under an emphatic horizontal roof and trellis, ornamented by blocks of wood painted red to accent the blue-stained trim. Major rooms are located halfway between the two bedrooms below and the two above; the bedroom roof level is continued over the dining room, library, and kitchen as a clerestory (Fig. 35). From the living room, at the right, the house is stepped back to the large dining room window and finally to the two levels of bedrooms. The skylight at the chimney lights both the living room and the library (Fig. 36).

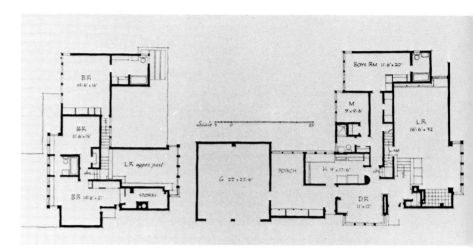

39

Alden W. Hanson house, Midland, 1934. The planting is included in a composition of geometry and vegetation, color and texture. The high volume of the living room (Fig. 39) is contrasted with an inglenook elaborated within the three-foot unit system that aligns the concrete blocks.

37

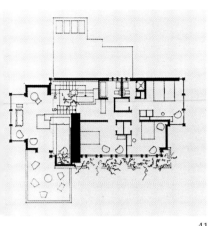

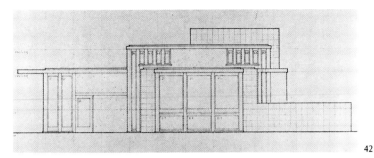

42

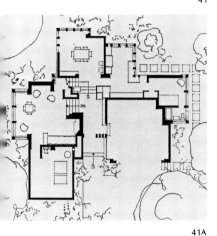

41

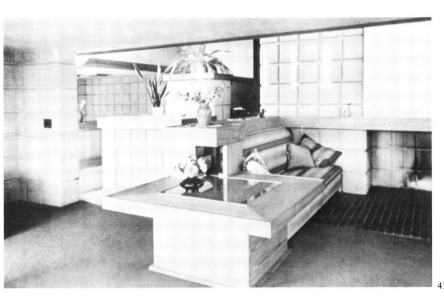

43

41A

40

John S. Whitman house, Midland, 1934. The quiet, layered entrance elevation (Fig. 40) belies an intricate, five-level interior. The design won the grand prize for residential architecture at the Paris Exposition of Arts and Technology in 1937. In the plans and elevation (Figs. 41–42) a five-foot unit system arranges the spiral of levels around a stair. The roof of the top level bedrooms is common to the living room clerestory in front of the chimney. The dining room at the left and the living room also share the same roof, though their floor levels differ by four and a half feet. The view from the living room (Fig. 43) is toward the stair to the bedrooms and down to the dining room, visible to the left. The glass-topped table conceals lights which cast shadows of the leaves, flowers, or swimming fish in the bowls set on it.

Charles MacCallum house, Midland, 1935. The living room is backed by the carefully composed mantel and upstairs overlook as it opens through the large windows accented by red squares of glass.

48

47

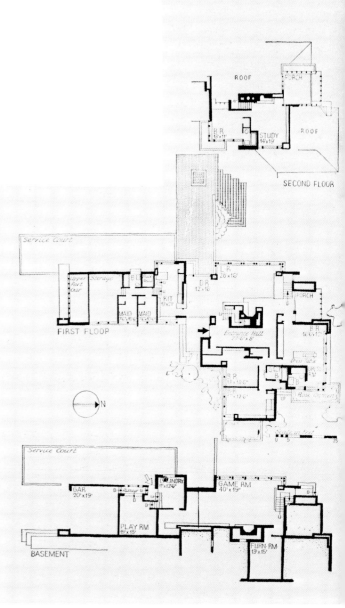

This plan developed extensions like those of the Stein house from an earlier, more compact plan. Brick paving flows from the entrance through the house past the hearth, up to the guest hall, and out again onto both levels of the screened porch.

The low entrance facade of the MacCallum house (Fig. 45) gives no hint of the garden side (Fig. 46), with its extended walls and roofs and the airy volume of the porch, screened at top and sides.

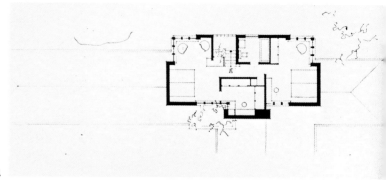

49A

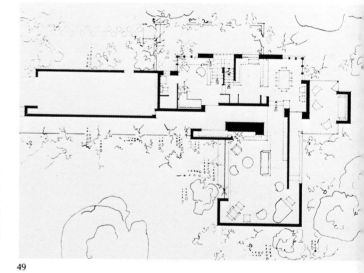

Oscar C. Diehl house, Midland, 1935. The plan arrangement and spreading roofs (Fig. 49) extend it beyond its two-bedroom program. The brick and diamond-leaded windows recall the Towsley house of three years earlier, but the extended eaves and asymmetric wall arrangement (Fig. 50) suggest the Stein house two blocks away. A familiar contrast of smooth and rough textures is seen in the living room (Fig. 51).

49

50

51

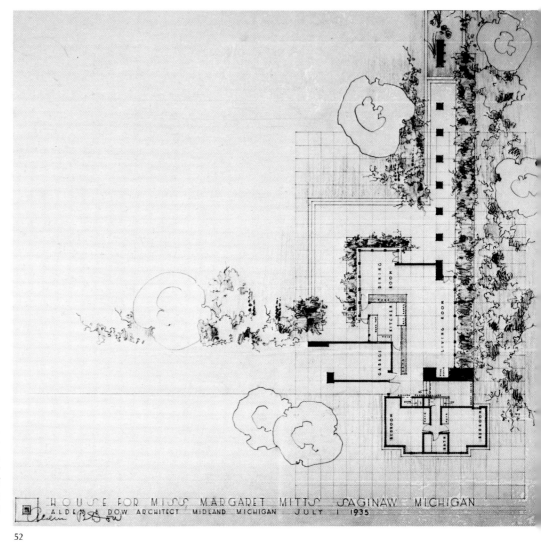

HOUSE FOR MISS MARGARET MITTS SAGINAW MICHIGAN
ALDEN B DOW ARCHITECT MIDLAND MICHIGAN JULY 1 1935

52

First project for Margaret Mitts house, Saginaw, 1935. This project is a stunning essay in lyrical spatial continuity. Bedrooms are separate, but all other living areas flow together around wooden casework. An exotic touch is given the drawing by coloring the Unit Blocks red-orange.

HOUSE FOR MISS MARGARET MITTS SAGINAW MICHIGAN
B DOW ARCHITECT

53

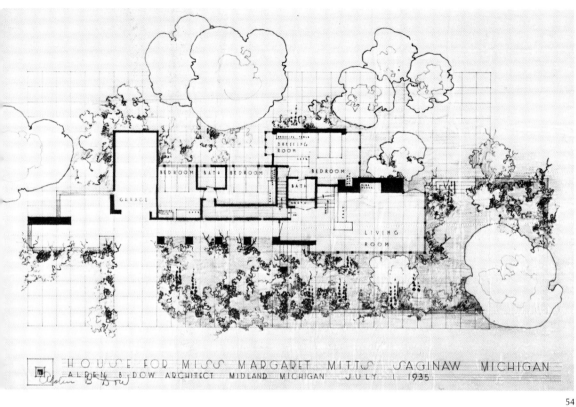

HOUSE FOR MISS MARGARET MITTS SAGINAW MICHIGAN
ALDEN B DOW ARCHITECT MIDLAND MICHIGAN JULY I 1935

54

cond project for Mitts house, 1935. A more complex spatial arrangement using a half-level
oduces an asymmetrical exterior massing anchored by the chimney, similar to the first
oject.

HOUSE FOR MISS MARGARET MITTS SAGINAW MICHIGAN
ALDEN B DOW ARCHITECT MIDLAND MICHIGAN JULY I 1935

55

Dow Chemical Company Main Office, Midland, 1935, entrance. This enlargement-remodeling was Dow's first major non-residential commission. The wide steps with illuminated glass block risers lead to a composition of simple brick volumes relieved by planting.

56

James T. Pardee house, Midland, 1936. The entrance terrace leads past the service wing on the right to the living room on the left.

58

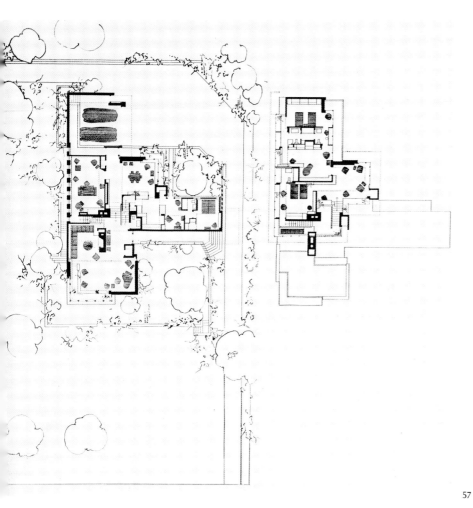

57

The Pardee design (Fig. 57) enlarges upon the split-level plans of
earlier houses. In a preliminary version the dining room had
overlooked the street, causing internal circulation problems. In
the final version (Fig. 59) one descends from the entrance-living
room level to the dining room or ascends to the sun room,
master bedroom suite, and guest room.

59

Mary Dow house, Saginaw, 1936. Dow screened his aunt's house, on a narrow city lot, by terraces raised behind generous planting boxes. The living room is overlooked by two bedrooms through hinged wooden panels and is ornamented by cypress and red glass. Glass block introduces light along the lot lines.

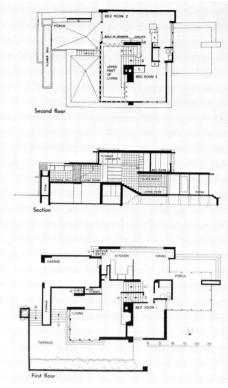

Second floor

Section

First floor

62

60

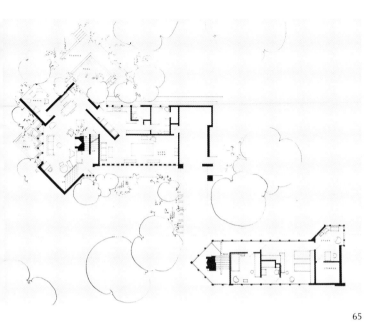

65

George Greene house, Midland, 1936. An unusual diagonally shingled exterior wall marks the diagonally placed living and dining rooms, whose windows repeat the angular motif with a saw-tooth projection into a small pool. The angle is turned at the mid-level entrance behind the chevron-ornamented fireplace.

64

63

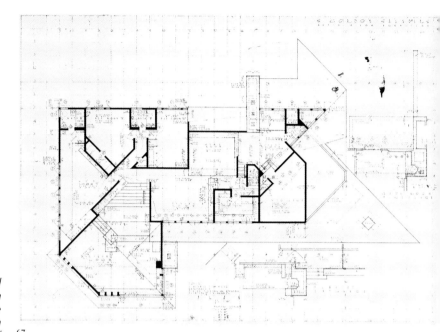

S. Gordon Saunders house, Bloomfield Hills, 1936. The red shingle roof spreads over the white plaster and cypress trim and down to the slightly sunken living room at the left. One enters beside the chimney after passing the raised kitchen and dining room level. Diagonal walls under the sloped roof conceal pipe columns to support steel beams spanning the irregular spaces. Wright is supposed to have said of this house, ''I think the boy went too far.''

67

66

Charles Bachman house, Lansing, 1937. The main living areas are raised one level above the street: living room to the left, dining room to the right behind the screened porch. Bedrooms extend to the rear.

68

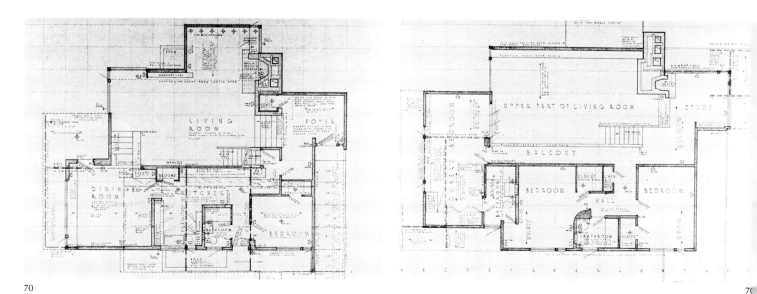

William K. Koerting house, Elkhart, Indiana, 1937. This house uses cypress trim and plaster to enclose a crisp assemblage of cubic masses. The mid-level living room (Fig. 70) opens to the river through an eleven-by-six-foot pane of glass.

69

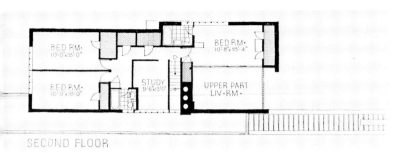

SECOND FLOOR

72

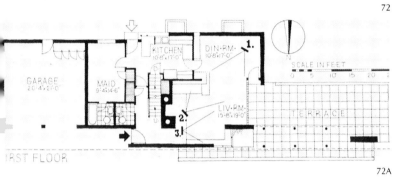

FIRST FLOOR

72A

73

llard Pryor house, Grosse Pointe Park, 1937. The European starkness of this
use was appreciated by critics who preferred the imported variety of modern
chitecture to the American. This design served as a legal test case as to whether
odern architecture could be zoned out of a neighborhood. The simple plan (Fig.
) is given variety by the double-height living room and a low entrance projected
the trellis. The unshielded expanse of glass block (Fig. 73) was to be shaded by
willow.

71

Dow Chemical exhibit, Golden Gate Exposition, San Francisco, 1939 (Fig. 75). The new plastic sheets were used to create this exhibit. The project for the "1940" house, 1937 (Fig. 74), sheathed in one-foot-square plastic sheets, was an adaptation of Dow's Unit Block system to a modern material being developed by the Dow Chemical Company.

75

74

"HILLHOUSE" A HOUSE FOR MR & MRS K T KELLER
ALDEN B DOW ARCHITECT MIDLAND MICHIGAN NOVEMBER 1938

Project for K. T. Keller house, 1938. This is the second in a series of unbuilt projects. The first Hillhouse, with a copper roof, extended along the lake shore bluffs. Compare this flat-roofed scheme with Chrysler president Lynn Townsend's house of 1963 (Fig. 113).

78

79

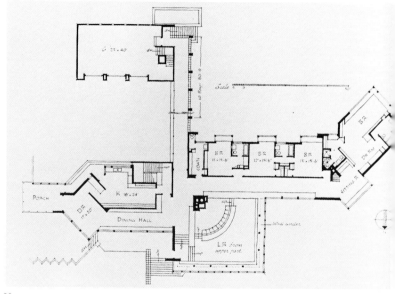

80

Anderson Arbury house, Midland, 1939. This strangely undomestic structure is
largest house thus far designed by Dow. The living room, screened by flank.
passages in casework, is on two levels: the lower one has built-in seating in an
around the fireplace; the higher level is that of the windows. Mirrors on the v
and ceiling of the dining room multiply the square grid, marked by small lights. T
cross-shaped plan separates the functions of each arm.

77

A. W. Hodgkiss house, Petoskey, 1939. One of Dow's last Unit Block houses, its spaces, all on one level, are less complex in their relationship than those of the earlier houses.

81

5. Reorientation in the Forties

The challenges and costs presented by the Unit Blocks made Dow look more favorably on simpler wood frame construction. In the seven years after he opened his practice in Midland, he built thirteen houses using the block, which became a kind of trademark. In the interest of flexibility and economy, he began exploring the use of frame and panel materials for textural contrast. This new expression of the principles of composition is evident in the Paul Rood house in Kalamazoo of 1938 and the Calvin Campbell house in Midland of 1939.

Rood contacted Dow in July, 1937, from Ann Arbor. He had seen the Towsley house there and had talked to an architecture student who had mentioned Dow. He also wrote to the Midland Chamber of Commerce for more information. The family was about to move to Kalamazoo, where Paul Rood had taken a teaching job. During the next several months, Dow and the Roods worked over the plans, trying, as Dow saw it, to resolve the conflict between cost and desire. Dow explained his concern for composition in a letter to Paul Rood when his drawings were finished. He thought that it would be a mistake to break up the living room window with a wall area because the effect was so fine and heat loss was not as serious as it might sound.[1] The flat roof, brick, and homosote panels divided by wood battens create a planar composition accentuated by a linear pattern emphasizing the four-foot unit system (Figs. 82-84).

Calvin Campbell was the general legal counsel to Dow Chemical. He had degrees from the University of Michigan, the MIT School of Business Administration, and the Harvard Law School. His house, like the Roods', is brick and homosote, but is sheltered by a hipped asbestos-shingle roof (Fig. 85). Entry is on the first level, which also includes a game room, kitchen, dining room (facing the street), and maid's quarters. After ascending a broad stair, one arrives behind the fireplace of the living room, which faces away from the street (Fig. 86). A study is located over the dining room. Three bedrooms are aligned alongside the two major second-floor rooms. The Campbell house was one of the few houses that Dow designed before World War II with hot-water heat.

In both these houses Dow again uses mirrors to expand interior space (his most elaborate use of the device was on the walls and ceiling of the Arbury dining room). The Rood house has a large mirror over the dining room cabinets; in the Campbell house there is a large mirror over the built-in seat perpendicular to the fireplace.

Two years after the design for the Koerting house in Elkhart, Dr. Millard Fleming had Dow design a flat-roofed house almost directly across the St. Joseph River from the Koertings (Fig. 87). Although Dr. Fleming liked the Unit Blocks and was willing to have them used (he had seen them in the Midland Chamber of Commerce booklet, which included a view of Dow's studio), brick was finally chosen for the masonry. The house was built by the contractor who had done Koerting's house, with wood siding replacing the stucco panels of an earlier scheme.

In line with the simplification evident in these two houses, Dow designed several Midland homes in 1940 of less distinctive design. The Reinke, Buntschoen, and Mac-Martin houses are pleasant but nothing out of the mainstream of Dow's work. The Leo B. Grant house was a single-level development of the Cavanagh house for the manager of the Dow Metal (magnesium) division of Dow Chemical. The MacMartin house, a further development of the F. W. Lewis house, was built for $7,500 by the ABD Building Co. MacMartin, who was a local clothier, also asked Dow for a design for his store.

The Grant house was one of the first houses built by the Alden B. Dow Building Company. In the February 18, 1941, issue of the *Weekly Bulletin* of the Michigan Society of Architects, Dow, a director of the society at the time, urged architects to master the facts of production, price, and availability of materials: "If we are going to be leaders of the building profession, we must contribute to its growth, not through the medium of laws, but through the medium of ability and practice. To some, this idea may appear to be digressing from the ethics of the profession, but it must be realized that when ethics cease to be strengthening, they no longer have value."[2] Dow used the design-build arrangement on several Midland projects until about 1950, at which time the American Institute of Architects became concerned with those potential conflict-of-interest problems, and Dow accordingly abandoned the practice.

If the Rood and Campbell houses are simplified adaptations of earlier houses, the Don Irish and Shailer Bass houses of 1941 are substantially new. They have neither flat nor hipped roofs, but simple asymmetrical gable roofs which top off plaster or brick walls. These wall surfaces are interrupted by carefully composed bands or banks of windows in the larger rooms. The Irish house (Fig. 88) is entered on the lower level, which contains the dining room, kitchen and game room, all opening on ground-level terraces. Dow discussed the design of the house in the same terms he had used in 1934 and 1935: "Softness balances hardness, smoothness balances roughness, plainness balances pattern, one color balances another color. Spaces are seldom definitely defined and all parts are correlated and serve a purpose."[3] Although the principles at work may be the same, the expression of them is less distinct than in earlier houses. One of the paradoxes about designing houses is that the architect wants to give people something which looks ahead, something to grow into, while at the same time providing a setting for the important fact of the building: the people in it and their present lives. Now the latter goal began to take priority in the design process. Both Irish and Bass were chemists at Dow Chemical, and their houses are next to each other to the west of the Midland Country Club.

A second significant new direction began with the thirty-five-hundred-square-foot house for Dr. and Mrs. John Grebe, seven miles west of Midland. The house is almost square, arranged in a nave-side aisle configuration with the living room and porch-greenhouse in the nave position. One "aisle" is comprised of a barracks-like row of six bedrooms and three bathrooms, separated by dressing rooms which are reached through doors opening directly from the central space. The other "aisle" contains dining room, kitchen, maid's bedroom, entry, coal bin, and garage. The section reflects the three-part division, with a low pitch over the central living space. This plan and section were to be developed in many ways in subsequent houses. The structure of the house is based on a unit system of thirty-two inches, with four-by-four-inch studs supporting homosote panels for both interior and exterior walls. Joists, also four by four, were seven feet eight inches off the floor. The first proposal for the house in May, 1941, was based on the familiar four-foot units. Its plan arrangement, though elongated, is continued in the July working drawings using the smaller unit system. The living room projects beyond the body of the house in an off-center angle which creates a moment of surprising irregularity in the midst of insistent modularity.

John Grebe came to the United States from Germany in 1914. After attending Case Institute, he moved to Midland to work for the chemical company. There he was recognized as an eccentric genius. He commissioned another house from Dow in 1958, which went through many phases as experiment succeeded experiment.

The first church Dow designed was for the Reorganized Church of Latter Day Saints in Midland in 1941. Its rectangular volume is enlivened by ornamental recessed panels flanking the front door (Fig. 89). In 1958 a garden court was added between the sanctuary and new classrooms and offices. The woodwork of chancel and entrance is an expansion of the shelving of the earlier houses with the added emphasis befitting their communal setting. The heavy wooden door pulls are in scale with the whole entry composition; their softly rounded form is comfortable for human hands.

Dow's designs for small houses began with the F. W. Lewis house, designed in 1933. In 1935 he developed two simple flat-roofed boxes twenty feet wide, using some of his Unit Blocks (Fig. 90). These three-bedroom houses were forty feet long; the four-bedroom ones were forty-six feet long. The site plan, with a density of 3.3 units per acre, arranged twelve units with large gardens on a block 580 by 270 feet. The houses are oriented not toward the street but toward an internal set of driveways and alleys in which every four units share garages and a laundry. A note along the sixty- and eighty-foot rights-of-way indicates that this pattern could continue at the rate of eight blocks per mile in the long direction and twelve blocks per mile in the short direction. The effect of several miles of such houses, even as attractive as these, might have been less impressive than the architect anticipated.

Dow realized that the Unit Block, however successful it might be in creating effective compositions in these basic housing projects, also raised the cost, and in his subsequent low-cost housing plans he used the wallboard panel and batten system first found in his studio drafting room and in the Lewis house. He also designed a simple two-bedroom house in 1937 for the Reverend A. C. Barclay, Mrs. Dow's grandfather (Fig. 91).

85

In February of 1939, a group of promoters from Detroit asked Dow to participate in the Ingleside Housing Project. Five hundred houses were to be built near Mt. Clemens, on land being sold by Detroit Creamery Farms. Wallbridge, Aldeinger and Company were to be engineers and contractors. Dow supplied them with eight housing types, priced from $3,800 to $4,800. Both flat and pitched roofs sheltered wallboard walls divided by batten strips and casement windows. In July, 1939, Dow's office worked up red poché plans and colored pencil perspectives.

By January of 1940, typical contractor details were ready. Announcements of the project listed 356 plots for initial development. An early site plan had arranged the small houses in circles "to cement a more neighborly feeling among the groups." There were difficulties in the coordination of all forces, including the market demand, the raising of money, and troublesome FHA size requirements. By February, Dow's interest was lagging. He realized that capturing people's imaginations with something new could not be done in the abstract. They would only be convinced if the houses were built first and sold later. "Trying to appeal to all of the sentimental tastes of the various buyers and at the same time produce a building that is superior is some job," he wrote.[4] He was working under more favorable conditions in a small housing project for Dow Chemical in Freeport, Texas. Finally, in May, he expressed his lack of enthusiasm for the Ingleside project, not only from a design standpoint but from the investment angle. He did not want to go through all that trouble just to "scrap with promoters."[5]

In 1939, he had worked up a complete wallboard and batten flat-roofed house "101" for the chemical company. He opened an office in Texas in 1941, and divided his activities between Texas and Midland until 1947, when the Texas office closed.

Dow first investigated the possibilities of the circle as architectural geometry in a Houston project in October of 1943. An employee of Dow's office in Houston remembers this project as a wonderful expression of Dow's quick mind and his delightful capacity for fantasy and humor.[6] The "House of Circles" was an amazing composition of almost complete circles which made up independent structures housing entrance gate and caretaker's cottage; garage and chauffeur's quarters; kitchen, dining room, and maid's room; living room; and a three-bedroom sleeping element (Fig. 92). In 1944, Dow responded to a request by John R. Donnell of Findlay, Ohio, for a double house by designing an elaborate, though more integrated, composition using circular forms. One entered between two opposing circular walls which led into a glass-walled link connecting the two residences; they overlooked a garden at the back. Over the next four years the project was developed into working drawings, as Dow and Donnell exchanged visits to Ohio and Midland. Dow asked to exhibit the plans in Ann Arbor at an architectural conference in February, 1945. A cost estimate of $200,000 in May, 1945, halted the initial project. A 1948 plan, more restrained, was Dow's last proposal in this sequence of unbuilt Donnell houses.

The Dow Chemical Company continued to investigate the potential for plastics and in 1946 planned to open a plastics sales office in a remodeled second-floor warehouse.

Dow proposed a design in which a carnival of curves demonstrated the possibilities of plastic. Along the edges of an area 120 by 50 feet, he distributed fourteen small interview booths shielded by curved partitions of woven plastic strips. Display areas were more elaborate demonstrations of curvilinear geometry, including kidney-shaped tables and shelving. Columns, ducts, and restrooms were camouflaged by curved elements. Offices were enclosed in cinderblock and plaster walls with large (eighteen-foot) radius curves. Both linoleum floor and ceiling were patterned in green and red, with the Dow Diamond corporate logo, very much like the San Francisco Dow exhibit.

A spiral design called the "Chrysler Carousel" was proposed by Dow in 1955 for a Chrysler showroom. The automobiles were to be spread out along a spiral display ramp. The circular plan was covered by a "spun dome," developed by the chemical company and used in classroom buildings at the Interlochen Academy in 1961 and at the Macromolecular Institute in Midland in 1970. Northwood Institute in Midland got a communication arts building in 1972, which Dow organized around a circular theme as well.

The opportunity to design larger community buildings marks a significant change in Alden Dow's architectural career around 1950. It is anticipated by the work he did in Lake Jackson, Texas, where a whole town was to be designed (see Chapter 7 below). In 1944, while he was in Texas, he entered a competition for the 36th Division Memorial (Fig. 93), a U.S. Army auditorium. The largest community building Dow built, the Midland Center for the Arts, more than twenty years later, owes much to this competition entry. On October 29, 1944, Dow was awarded the first prize of two thousand dollars by the sponsors, the Texas Society of Architects. The jury's comments show a somewhat surprising insight into the designer's compositional intentions. The scheme "grew on them," they said. It was "modern in feeling and simple in character, depending in the main on variations in wall surfaces to lend interest to the exterior."[7] Dow also explicitly linked visual forms to symbolic meanings: "Peace is generally regarded as a form of perfection. This is symbolized by the old symbol of perfection, the circle. In this building it takes on the form of a court open to the sky. Peace, or perfection, also represents freedom. Freedom in this building is illustrated by the openness of this court to the sky and more intimately by the freegrowing garden in the center."[8]

The Midland Hospital was designed in 1942. It is located in forty acres of woods northwest of the town. Dow described the single-level plan as having the advantage of allowing extension of bedroom facilities without disrupting the service facilities at the heart of the building.

Dow's principle of composition of sensory stimuli was used to good effect in this building. The occasional conflict between this principle and other requirements was pointed out in a *Pencil Points* article on the hospital in August, 1945. The entrance front of the building is composed of a pipe-column loggia on a three-step platform; it passes in front of a wall of windows at the entrance and a blank brick wall along the kitchen. The hospital superintendent felt that "any section of a hospital where people are working eight or more hours a day should have outside windows, particularly when the surroundings are attractive." (Some of the thrust of her criticism is lost when we note that the "surroundings" here are a parking lot.) But it is in the use of color that Dow's attempt to achieve sensory comfort is most striking. "Every room has its individual balanced color scheme. Colors used in bedrooms might be called 'soft,' but colors in public areas are as brilliant as possible and lend a very cheerful air to the whole building," said Dow.[9] The entrance lobby has orange-red linoleum floors, a red-and-white reception desk, bright green plaster walls, and a cream ceiling. Light wood furniture is upholstered in yellow. Doors to bedrooms are painted pink, light blue, pastel green, or cream. The large windows in these rooms allow the forest, which is left wild, to become part of the room.

As World War II drew to a close, Dow actively participated in the production of badly needed housing. The Ingersoll Steel and Disc Division of Borg-Warner Corporation had developed a utility unit that could be set into a house to provide heating, toilet, and kitchen facilities. Ingersoll invited eight architects to design houses in Hillside Park on the Kalamazoo city line. J. Fletcher Lankton, who had worked on the utility core, L. Morgan Yost and George Fred Keck of Illinois, Harwell Hamilton Harris from California, and Hugh Stubbins, Jr., and Royal Barry Wills from the East Coast all participated. Dow and Stubbins designed two houses in a cul-de-sac driveway. Dow's hopes for low-cost housing were more nearly fulfilled by these demonstration houses financed by industry than they were in the Ingleside venture. He wrote to the organizer of the project: "As I said last spring, I think the important thing in housing is to show people how to play with small houses. It is also important to consider the fact that few people buy a minimum house, or at least, few want to buy minimum. They are looking for ideas, and the more we can show them in this house, the happier they are going to be with LAUNKITCHEATOIL,"[10] the last term Dow's humorous word for the ingenious Ingersoll utility unit. As is often the case with industrialized building prototypes, problems arose not so much in fitting it all together as in trying to service or adapt a tightly integrated package with the passage of time.

Dow took the plans for his basic two-bedroom and expanded three-bedroom houses to the project organizer in New York at the beginning of July. Three weeks later he was informed that they ran over the intended budgets of $5,500 and $8,500. There was also careful figuring of heat loss, which was not to exceed 70,000 and 122,000 BTU's per hour. From the beginning, Dow was thinking in terms of cost-cutting through some degree of pre-cut or prefabrication on the order of the Homosote Precision Build methods, which interested him greatly. In December, 1945, he described the house and the reasons for its design features, which included an efficient, square plan sheathed in asbestos, an increase in effective interior space by means of outward-sloping windows to front and rear, and a concentration of window and wall areas on the exterior to make an effective background for landscaping (Fig. 94). He concluded his description by saying: "I think the most an architect can say for a house is that I would enjoy living in it."[11]

Dow also prescribed the interior colors and selected movable furniture from Herman Miller and Artek. Living, dining, and kitchen floors were blue linoleum; a large table top was red linoleum; the desk top and eating counter were green enamel. A birch dining table had yellow leather chairs around it. The red-green and yellow-blue contrasts are evident in these color schemes.

A model of the house was built, and was covered at length in the February, 1946, *Architectural Forum*[12] and at the National Association of Home Builders in Chicago in March.

A second industrial house project came from the Libby-Owens-Ford program of solar homes for each of the forty-eight states. Dow designed the Michigan solar house in the fall of 1945. Early studies in October worked off the curved forms for the Donnell house, which were on the boards at the time. The south wall was a simple concave, then a segmental curve in glass, and then became a more complex pair of quarter-circles integrated with a curved pool. A December scheme which was later developed into working drawings in 1947 showed a two-story porch and a living room thermo-pane wall to the south; a shed roof sloped to one-story level at a kitchen and entry; bedrooms projected in a line off the higher volume.[13] Curiously, Harwell Hamilton Harris' solar house for California looks more like Dow than Dow does.

Dow was an unsuccessful entrant in a *Pencil Points* 1944 competition in association with Pittsburgh Plate Glass for "A House for Cheerful Living." The results were presented in the May, 1945, issue. The winning entry was a design from Birmingham, Michigan, by Fletcher and Fletcher. The competitors were free to choose the locale for their "cheerful" house, and Dow, working in Houston, chose the southwest. As he had in the Ingersoll house, he used outward-sloping glass with awning sash and mirrored sills added. All three of these industry houses were significant departures from the forms Dow had used so successfully for years. As a result they are not so surely composed, as he attempts to integrate technological gadgets of one sort or another. The machine analogy of modernism was never congenial to Dow, and when he tried to adapt that image, his own strengths were compromised.

In October, 1945, as a development of his interest in panelized wall construction, Dow was working on the construction and joint details of a sandwich panel, which were applied to a refrigerator for Chrysler the next year. These panels were revived in 1952 and used in construction of two houses in Midland.

In 1946 Dow was working on a house for Dr. Fred Olsen of Alton, Illinois. Olsen worked for Olin Industries, where he was developing an Industrial Research Institute with an interest in creativity both scientific and artistic (Olsen had studied painting with Hans Hoffmann). Before the war Dow had designed a large house arranged around a motor-entrance court; the house reached into the twenty-five-acre site by means of extensive trellises along walls enclosing gardens. The Olsens visited Midland in 1946 to pick up the interrupted project and to see Dow's own house, which had then been completed. While Dow was designing a smaller house for the woods, Olsen was looking at a dramatic site beside an old quarry in Connecticut, where he was relocating his research facilities. Dow kept up with this fitful client at least in part because of the opportunity to work in such an interesting location. By January, 1948, *Architectural Forum* had got wind of the quarry house and was interested in publishing it when it was built.[14] Olsen ultimately did not build Dow's grand design because he felt it was not appropriate to the neighborhood or the tradition of modest residences for Olin employees. There was an opportunity to involve other artists in the houses, which made the project even more attractive. Hillis Arnold, the ceramist from Cranbrook, was brought to Midland to discuss the place of sculpture, and the painter Hans Moller was mentioned.

Dow wrote to Arnold and, by way of introducing him to his thoughts, talked of the role of sculpture within architecture. He began with the general principle that "man builds in order to satisfy his needs. These needs are first physical. He must have protection from the heat and cold; from the storms." A building is "a barrier to intruders; it is a place for privacy. In addition to these, it is a place that makes life easier and more enjoyable." The next category of needs he related to the exercise of the senses: "we must have balance in color, balance in form, balance in space and feel, and so on. Textures must offer the same balance with plain surfaces. There must be intricate patterns balanced with plain surfaces. There must be colored patterns balanced with plain patterns."[15]

After setting the stage, Dow addressed the role that sculpture could play:

> It is in these two fields [physical and sensuous] that sculpture becomes important, for these patterns, when formed by man, can add an intellectual quality to that surface. It is important that this quality be a natural part of the building, for the intellect demands naturalness. The building must be considered as a planned effort striving first to take care of the physical needs and finally the intellectual needs. These intellectual needs in their highest form should be inspirations to do more on the part of those that use the building. In other words, the more we can make Mr. Olsen think and do things to this building himself, the more successful it will be.[16]

The notion that his building is to be a model that will influence those within it to act in accordance with its standard is one that Dow has stated again and again. When the inhabitants' responses are sufficiently sensitized to achieve harmony with the setting Dow provides, then they can participate in shaping that environment. Their innate capacity for finer feelings, in which Dow firmly believed, can be measured by the completeness of their understanding of the architecture around them. Before they achieve that total harmony, or should it become evident that they are unable to do so, they are to ask Dow for guidance.

The most public house Dow would design was the governor's residence in Lansing, Michigan. He expressed interest in the project in January, 1946, and by July had a preliminary plan, drawn in red poché and colored pencil. It presented a rather predictable one- and two-story house, an enlarged version of which contained three hundred thousand cubic feet. Its general appearance, according to Dow, "should not be stiff and domineering, but rather a fine expression of naturalness in living."[17] In addition to an office suite, the house had the usual residential rooms, though on a much enlarged scale, as befitted a semi-public place. The goal toward which Dow was striving—naturalness—seemed to elicit negative responses. Responses offered when the model was on display included "it looks like a ranch house" or "it belongs in California."[18] The red walls and green roof also disturbed some people. Cost estimates for the brick house, with a copper roof over gypsum plank on steel and oak woodwork, approached $350,000. The unenthusiastic public response, in addition to some wrangling over what percentage the architect would get for this state building, finally called the whole project to a halt. It terms of its importance to Dow's architectural expression, this project does not bulk large, despite its size and public nature.

If Dow did not get the chance to design the quarry house for the Olsens in 1947, he did begin work on a house on the stone foundations of a barn on Altepec Hill overlooking the Brandywine River near Chadds Ford, Pennsylvania, north of Wilmington, Delaware. W. Hale Charch, who worked for the rayon division of Du Pont, was a distant relative of Dow's by marriage. As a result of a fire, Charch needed a new house; he asked Dow to design a building using the native stone from the hillside behind the old foundation. In November, 1947, Dow wrote Charch enclosing the plans and explaining how he envisioned the flat-roofed house as it stretched along the hill, its major rooms in a line looking out of large windows between stone walls and piers. He described a version which preserved the redwood fascia, random masonry, and window areas of an earlier proposal (but did not revive his earlier suggestion that Charch and his wife participate in finishing the house by making carvings in the stones of the walls). The Charchs moved into their house in April, 1950.

The important public building that heralded an increasing emphasis on community structures after 1950 was the outstanding First Methodist Church for Midland, whose red poché plan and colored pencil perspective were drawn in May, 1947. The nave-side aisles section used in the Grebe house is here applied to a genuinely ecclesiastical structure (Figs. 95–98). The building, opened in September, 1950, was given an Award of Merit by the American Institute of Architects in 1956.

By 1949, Alden Dow had received considerable exposure and praise in both the professional and the popular press. In the March 15, 1948, issue of *Life*, five pages, including full-color pages, were devoted to his work. The subtitle of the article, "His Modern Homes Are Not Monastic," drew attention to the acceptability of his work:

In their unrelenting march away from traditionalism, modern architects too often achieve cold, logical efficiency at the expense of the qualities which make a house inviting and warmly livable. One U.S. architect whose houses are not merely efficient, but thoroughly livable is Alden Dow. His style grows out of a deep conviction that man's emotional requirements in architecture are as vital as his material ones. . . . As a result Dow never begins a house without making an unusually painstaking study of the needs and personalities of the family that will occupy it.

The results, said *Life*, "are always original and possess an informal charm that makes them some of the most satisfying residences in the U.S." [19] The houses illustrated included his own home, the Saunders house, and the Campbell house, all of them designed before the war. Dow was led to believe that the *Life* team that stayed in Midland for several days would produce a more representative selection of his work, but this did not happen. At any rate, the article offered him an opportunity to pause for reflection in mid-career.

Dow was forty-five. He had lived in his newly completed home only part of each year from 1941 to 1947. His architectural practice would not again have the small home-town focus it had when he was younger. The coming years would require adjustments on both personal and professional fronts. The challenge was to go beyond what he had already done. Dow is not a man to rest on his laurels, but the next step was not to be an easy one.

Notes

1. Letter of May 31, 1938.

2. "The Master Builder," M.S.A. *Weekly Bulletin*, February 18, 1941, p. 1.

3. "Evolution of a Design," in Walter A. Taylor, ed., *1948 Convention Seminars, Addresses & Discussions on Aesthetics, Urban Planning, Dwellings, Retail Business Buildings, Modular Designs* (Washington, D.C., 1948), pp. 24–28.

4. Letter to W. D. Guy, February 5, 1940.

5. Letter to Ted Anderson, May 13, 1940.

6. Personal communication to the author, Houston, Texas, May 30, 1979.

7. Quoted in M.S.A. *Weekly Bulletin*, November 14, 1944, p. 15.

8. Quoted in *Architectural Forum*, March, 1945, p. 82.

9. "Midland Hospital," *Pencil Points*, August, 1945, pp. 56–66.

10. Letter to Ralph G. Gulley, September 19, 1945.

11. Letter to Bruce Biosset, December 1, 1945.

12. "Five Houses," *Architectural Forum*, February 1946, pp. 92–93.

13. Maron J. Simon, ed., *Your Solar House* (New York, 1947).

14. Dow to Fred Olsen, January 12, 1948.

15. Letter to Hillis Arnold, June 29, 1948.

16. *Ibid.*

17. Letter to Adrian Langius, November 27, 1946.

18. Governor's Residence job file, Alden B. Dow Associates.

19. "Architecture: Alden Dow: "His Modern Homes Are Not Monastic," *Life*, March 15, 1948, pp. 88–92.

Reorientation in the Forties / ILLUSTRATIONS

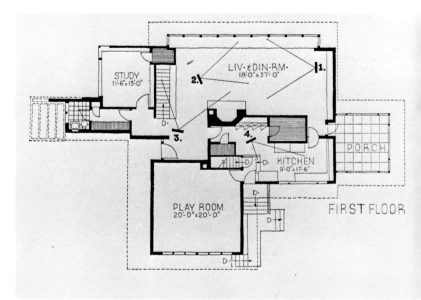

83

84

Paul Rood house, Kalamazoo, 1938. This is an example of the brick and panel construction Dow used when he abandoned the Unit Blocks. Living and dining rooms are upstairs, bedrooms below. Ornamental texture is confined to the ceiling and the row of brass lights over the fireplace.

82

Calvin Campbell house, Midland, 1939. Although larger than Rood's, an increasing simplicity of interior and exterior surfaces is evident. The dining room is at entrance level, the living room upstairs.

86

Millard Fleming house, Elkhart, Indiana, 1939. The entrance and living room of this riverfront house are on the middle level. As in the Koerting house across the river (Fig. 69), the entrance side is enlivened by a composition of overhangs and receding wall planes.

Don Irish house, Midland, 1941. This is Dow's first use of a single-gable roof. Its two-level arrangement is made more dramatic by a stair up to the living room and a balcony overlooking the high-ceilinged dining room.

88

Reorganized Church of Latter Day Saints, Midland, 1941. A simple rectangular volume is embellished by crisply outlined projecting windows, a recessed doorway, and a chimney-tower. The carved frieze beside the doorway was completed by the congregation.

A. C. Barclay house, Midland, 1937. In this compact low-cost house, window areas contrast with blank walls under a roof without overhang, much like the F. W. Lewis house of 1933 (Figs. 29–31).

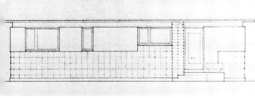

90

...ject for low-cost housing, 1935. The roof of this ...ee-bedroom prototype is cantilevered on two-by-...s spiked to the joists. The cinderblock wall is a ...tern of standard smooth blocks and windows ...ve the beveled Unit Blocks.

91

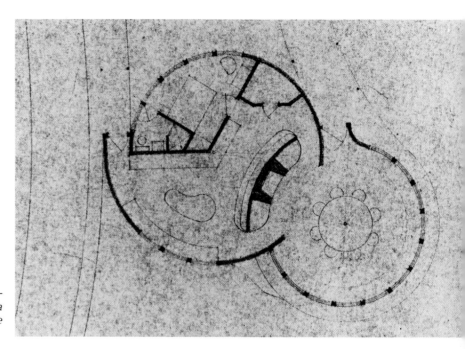

Project for "House of Circles," 1943. This plan distributes various functions along covered walkways in a demonstration of ingenuity with the compass. The pavilion shown is the dining area.

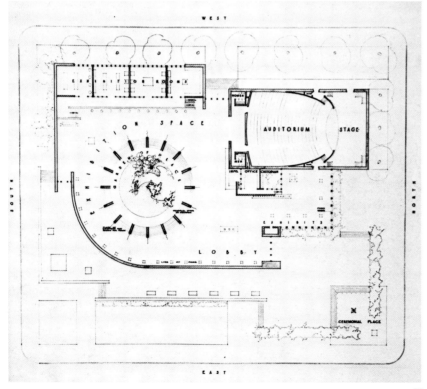

Project for 36th Division Memorial, 1944. Dow's winning en in the anonymous competition surrounded an outdoor gard with an exhibition space decorated by flags.

93

Ingersoll demonstration house, Kalamazoo, 1945. Outward-sloping windows and mirrors on internal walls expand the compact living areas surrounding one of the company's utility units.

94

Reorientation in the Forties

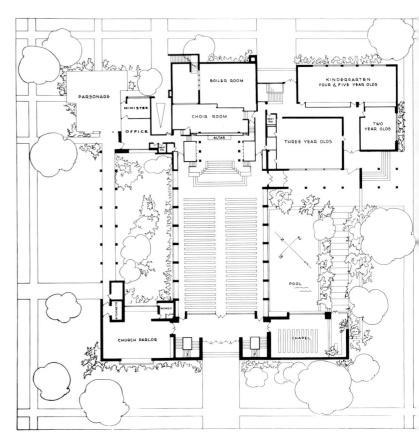

First Methodist Church, Midland, 1947. This important communal structure was dedicated in 1950. Color contrast is achieved with orange brick and verdigris copper. Extensive planting boxes on the building contrast with sharp-edged architectural geometry (Fig. 95). Patterns of brick wall planes and light are focused on the chancel, which is illuminated by a skylight (Fig. 96). In 1952 a chapel (Fig. 98) and classrooms under the pool (Fig. 97) were added; the second courtyard was enclosed in 1967. The shallow pool reflects the patterns of colored glass squares and ornamental foliage.

96

98

6. Architectural Work after 1950

By 1949 Dow had gained national recognition for a body of architectural work governed by a set of thoughtful principles. That was not a good year for him otherwise, however. A direct clash with Frank Lloyd Wright occurred early in the year over the Phoenix Civic Center. When the Phoenix group approached Wright regarding the commission, he responded with a vision of such magnificence and expense that the city fathers backed down. Though they were not willing to wait while building up the municipal coffers to finance the proposal of this architectural genius and neighbor, they respected the tradition established by Wright and looked around for an architect who would work within the scale they established but who was in the design tradition they admired. Alden Dow was that man.

Dow agreed to design, on the block-square site, a complex of library, auditorium, and museum. When the Taliesin group found out what had happened, they were outraged. Both Wright and Mrs. Wright accused Dow of ingratitude, unreliability, and professional undercutting. Wright was disappointed and distant; Olgivanna Wright was considerably more upset. Two months after this attack, Alden's older brother, Willard, who directed the chemical company, was killed with his wife in a plane crash. Later in the year Elzie Cote, who had been supervisor of the Dow gardens since 1906 and had worked closely with Dow's father in his landscape designs, also died, another personal blow for Dow.

Dow's 1949 design for the Phoenix Civic Center grouped library, little theater, museum, and support facilities around a square interior court whose landscaping included a pool (Fig. 99). The entrance is from the east, along Central Avenue, up broad steps through a colonnade of piers covered in decorative pre-cast panels. The garden was initially laid out in a free-form curvilinear composition, with the water forming an irregular band along the colonnade. In 1954 the museum building was added to the library and little theater. Associated architects for the first phase were Lescher and Mahoney, for the second phase, Blaine Drake. The museum, which had come in over budget and had to be cut back, was enlarged in 1964.

In July of 1950 Dow's chief draftsman, Robert Goodall, left him. Goodall was born in Oak Park, Illinois, in 1904, studied journalism briefly at the University of Illinois in 1922, and, after working for various Chicago architectural firms, including Graham Anderson Probst and White, went to work with Wright. At Taliesin he was on the professional staff that helped instruct the Fellowship apprentices who arrived in the fall of 1932. When Wright was asked about Goodall in 1958, he is reported to have said, "The best draftsman I ever saw, but never an architect."[1] He was the chief draftsman for the Willey house of 1932. Wright is said to have asked him to help with the manuscript of his *Autobiography* because Goodall's wide reading and mastery of the English language was a prominent facet of his quick, warm personality.[2]

Goodall joined Dow's Midland firm early in 1934. It was he who maintained close contact with Taliesin, particularly through Edgar Tafel. His ability to conceive and transfer intricate construction details to paper was outstanding. The sheets detailing the skylight at the chimney of his own house are magnificent: a complete visualization directly laid down in line work that eschews refinement of technique in favor of effective and convincing communication. Dow also used his graphic skills to carry on an experiment in colored line drawings to create the illusion of three dimensions.

Willard Fraser joined Dow and Goodall in Midland later in 1934. He came from Milwaukee but had known Goodall in Chicago. Reuben Pfeiffer joined the office early in 1935. "Tommy" Tompkins, who was the construction supervisor, and a secretary completed the original staff. A recent graduate of the University of Michigan, Frederick Graham, worked in the firm from July, 1936, to March, 1937. Later in 1936, Lee Cochran and Neil Warren were added, so that at the beginning of 1937 there were six draftsmen, Tompkins, and the secretary.[3]

Members of the Dow staff began to participate in community activities where they could contribute as artists and architects. In November, 1936, Willard Fraser gave a talk on architecture to the Tuesday Evening Lions Club. He was identified as an architect associated with the Alden B. Dow firm and as having recent experience in Chicago and Milwaukee. He commented that "prefabrication will not offer the Utopia that is perhaps hoped for it due to the fact that this type of material is used only in the shell of a house, and this in reality embraces only about 25% of the entire cost."[4] Pfeiffer, who later went to Texas with Dow and remained there, independently remodeled the University Club Rooms on Main Street in 1936, and Goodall served as a judge in the Rotary Club annual art exhibit at the Community Center the next year.[5] This kind of independence was not encouraged at the Dow office, however. Dow is said to have wanted to run the office as a business, and yet was uncomfortable at any mention of his own wealth or at talk of money in general.

Goodall married a Midland girl, Frances Mode, in August, 1935, and they soon moved into a lovely small house he designed, next door to her family. Goodall disagreed with Dow about the virtue of painting the Unit Blocks. He felt they should be left "natural" as they came from the forms. Dow's firm preference for finish to his materials contrasts with Wright's emphasis on naturalism, and besides, the natural dark gray blocks did not reveal their grid pattern so clearly as ones painted white, a feature important to Dow. As the postwar years unfolded, tensions developed in the studio which finally resulted in Goodall's departure in the summer of 1950. Until his death four years later at the age of fifty, he worked on his own projects around the area. They are characterized by a wonderful sense of detail, but without Dow's overall plan they tend not to hang together as total compositions.

A quite different personality who began affecting the work in the office around 1950 was an energetic 1948 graduate of the College of Architecture at the University of Michigan, Harvey "Cle" Allison. Over the next twenty years, Allison directed the office toward operations and commissions that had more to do with getting on in the world of business than with Dow's architectural principles.

These personal crises in 1949 and 1950 contributed significantly to a shift in the character of Dow's work. There was an increase in commissions for larger, public buildings. The philosophy of design Dow had developed and used in the beautiful domestic work of the thirties and forties was applied directly to these more complex functions. A less selective clientele cared less about balancing psychological responses in the face of tight budgets, and Dow's method of compositional contrasts was not readily adaptable to a structure that could not be thoroughly analyzed by means of an image. The private house or small church or library, on the other hand, lent itself readily to such an understanding (Figs. 100–101). Dow has great facility in sketching out a tiny plan so accurately to scale that it can be enlarged directly with almost no adjustment. His mastery of proportional relations of a certain size is remarkable. In the interest of getting on to the phase of designing smaller compositional features, he often short-circuited the more abstract, intellectual analysis of larger projects.[6] The importance of the design-development phase of the architect's work increases with the complexity of the building, and it was this crucial step that tended to be slighted, both because of Dow's interest in the smaller-scale elements and because of the firm's new emphasis on a rather raw idea of business efficiency, as advocated by Allison. Broad expanses of materials such as brick or stucco reduced the masses of larger buildings to a simple geometry of planes. A period known in the office as the "Deep Frieze Era" set in, as many buildings were terminated at the top by deep bands of wood, plaster, porcelain steel, or pre-cast concrete.

That is not to say Dow gave up his earlier mastery of contrasts entirely. By 1954, he had designed five significant churches in Midland whose ritual requirements could be effectively enhanced by his principle of contrast in equilibrium. The St. John's Episcopal Church, designed in late 1949 and early 1950 (Figs. 102–3), fits into its slightly sloping site with a central-gabled nave originally outlined with a copper fascia much like the First Methodist Church (see Figs. 95–98). In 1952 a rectory was designed behind the fellowship hall whose series of low gables rose above one side of the garden court. Acceding to the congregation's wish, the choir was placed on either side of the chancel rather than across the back, as it is in the First Methodist Church.

In January of 1953, Dow had designed the basic form of St. John's Lutheran Church for Midland. He centered the remarkable sanctuary on the altar. The roof form flared up in two layers of radiating gables, suggesting a number of symbolic references to a rose, a fortress to protect the altar, or even a Japanese fan opened to form a circle (Figs. 104–5). As with the previous congregations, Dow worked attentively to understand their ideas while expanding their own powers of imagination by his suggestions.[7]

One of the more intriguing applications of triangular patterns is found in the earliest proposals for the Bay City Jewish Center. A December, 1955, study used the Star of David as the plan form. In March of the next year, the star had been transformed to a novel section and elevation. The plan became a long rectangle with entry at one end and *bimah* at the other. One point of the star projected above the *bimah* as a kind of steeple. The roof of the main seating areas was flat; the walls sloped inward from both ceiling and floor to form the other four points of the star. By July of 1956, a much simpler orthogonal plan of brick and stucco topped by a heavy, ribbed fascia had appeared. In 1958 a precast concrete and glass screen was added at one corner in a diagonally arranged seating area.

The wide bands of fascia above brick walls also appeared in Christ Episcopal Church in Adrian (Fig. 106). Its earliest plan employed a diagonally oriented sanctuary in a square scheme in which a court was enclosed by rows of classrooms. In the final version of April, 1959, the diagonals are gone, and the design is characterized by extended plaster friezes and a high, flat-topped sanctuary.

In a variation of the gabled-nave, flat-side-aisle model, Dow used a barrel vault over the nave of the Hellenic Orthodox Community Church of St. George in Bloomfield Township. A brilliantly colored round window fitted into the ends of the semicircular vault. In 1952 the Presbyterians in Midland offered Dow the commission for a large structure for them, on the condition that it be in a colonial style. Dow declined, but now thinks that he would have liked such a challenge.

Dow's interest in the textural qualities of roof structure, first seen in the Heath house of 1934, reappears from time to time. One of the most interesting such expressions is a proposal which he first considered in 1955 but drew up the next year for the Homestyle Center Foundation. Arleigh C. Hitchcock, the executive director, was developing a demonstration village of twenty-five houses for various geographical regions around a pond at the edge of Grand Rapids. Included in the preliminary list of architects were Paul Rudolph, Buckminster Fuller, Harwell Hamilton Harris, Royal Barry Wills, Eliot Noyes, George Nelson, and Ralph Rapson, among others.[8]

In his two-story, fifty- by thirty-seven-foot house, Dow masterfully combined several characteristics of his earlier work. A two-story living room and entry stair behind a large brick chimney occupied the middle third of the house. A carport and four bedrooms, two on each side, were on the upper entrance level. Dining room, kitchen, and other living spaces were below the bedrooms. Three levels of four by twelves and four by tens created bands of exposed structure inside and out. The top level was exposed as a clerestory over the living room. Four-foot plastic panels separated the roof structure of the clerestory from the main roof. The roof edge was further articulated over each beam with a projecting metal cover plate. Inside, the upper-level balcony was defined at the top by the exposed ends of the main roof structure and below by the second-floor joists projecting two feet on center into the central space. The balcony posts were fixed in pairs on either side of the joists. The textural complexity along the edges of the high living space provides a fine example of how a structural necessity can be made to fulfill the sensory need for contrast, as the structure is played up against the simple brick chimney at one end and the window wall at the other. The bedrooms were separated from the balcony by sliding doors of wood and plastic.

The John Reicker house of 1961 is another expression of structural texture. Although the design of this Midland house began on a rare example of a triangular grid, it was built on a square module (Figs. 107–8). Its single-level plan, centered on a sunken living room, owed much to the Grand Rapids project and ultimately to the Grebe house plan of twenty years earlier. This reassuring display of the skill evident in earlier years brings to mind the special conditions that surrounded those prewar houses. Mrs. Reicker is Dow's niece; the close personal attention and the means that were devoted to the earlier houses were again present in this commission.

The compact plans of the Reicker and Homestyle houses are a continuation of the early Unit Block houses. In contrast, in only a very few plans are lines of rooms arranged in a branching manner. This basically Arts and Crafts planning principle is given its clearest expression in Dow's own studio and house. Wright's work, as Dow saw it in 1933, presented a similar contrast between the spreading expanse of Taliesin and the concrete block houses and compact first Willey house.

A year after the Reicker house, Dow designed a house for his daughter and her family, Mr. and Mrs. Peter Carras. Its laminated roof framing is also on a four-foot unit system. Dow's continuing interest in landscape compositions is present in color pencil perspectives of the view of the garden through the living room windows. He provided a view for summer and one for spring to show alternatives of color and texture.

In March of 1962, Dow continued to show renewed interest in intricate carpentry with a set of wooden lanterns for *House Beautiful*, which published them and made the plans available to readers who requested them.[9] Dow was greatly aided in working out the details of construction for these lanterns, examples of which grace the outside of the Reicker house (Fig. 109), by Ted Gwizdala. Ted had assisted as a laborer in building the initial studio of 1935. Over time he had become a master carpenter, a model builder, and a permanent member of Dow's staff who was responsible for any specialty items included in the plans. He built crosses for churches, cabinets, doors— whatever carpentry had an important place in the harmony of contrasts Dow was composing.

The triangular form that first appeared for symbolic reasons in the section of the Bay City Jewish Center was used again in 1951 for a most successful **A**-frame house for Mrs. Josephine Ashmun, a longtime resident of Midland and skilled golfer. The house is located in a thick woods of pine and deciduous trees whose texture it complements (Fig. 110). A basically simple **A**-frame is adjusted, cut away, and glazed on vertical and sloping planes. The insertion of a second level is done in such a way as to enhance the sloping form by hanging a balcony over the living room on diagonal wooden plates (Fig. 111). Dow has solved all of the problems of useful head room and structural integrity with grace and ingenuity.

A further development of the **A**-frame was a "**W**-frame" that Dow proposed for two clients in 1955 and 1960. Both Nils Munson and John Collinson finally decided upon houses with more familiar roof forms. In 1961, Dow gave the Roscommon Congregational Church an adaptation of the **A**-frame in a simple and satisfying wood church whose steeple rises in a tall isoceles triangle (Fig. 112).

The chairman of Dow Chemical, Leland I. Doan, asked Dow to design a house in 1957. The first plan was a domestically scaled, flat-roofed brick house with a narrow wood fascia enlivened with dentils. As built, it achieved a more substantial expression by use of rough ashlar stone and sloping shingle roofs whose eaves end in slightly uplifted stucco soffits. The larger domestic scale is present everywhere—large platforms of space flow around and down to the living room and up broad steps to a family sitting room. Both spaces are dominated by imposing stone fireplaces. Even though some of the floors are polished flagstones, the whole house is supported on steel bar joists. Dow called on two craftsmen to embellish this house: Eugene Masselink from Taliesin contributed a mural of triangular mirrors, and Paul Tono, who had visited Midland at Herbert Dow's invitation in 1925, sent landscape plans and sketches in March of 1959. The Doan house is very close to the site Dow selected for his studio in 1934, though by 1957 the site was served by utilities. The large maple that appears in elevation studies is off one corner of the porch of the present house.

Another large house that gained notoriety for Dow was the Miner S. Keeler II house in East Grand Rapids, designed in 1958. It was given extensive coverage by *House Beautiful* in August, 1962.[10] Requests for information and even plans of the house came to the Dow Associates from such places as New York City, Houston, Texas, and even Bedford Place, London. The Keeler house is another example of total design. Dow designed the silk draperies in red and green, blue and yellow, and the dining room rug in red outlined at the edges in two bands of white. A preliminary plan focused various pitched-roofed wings on the living room fireplace, much like the Arbury house plan. As built, on the four-foot unit system, various flat roofs lead from entrance and bedrooms banked against a low hill to a higher playroom and living room.

When the president of Duke University, Douglas M. Knight, approached Dow in 1963 with a request for a home, Dow revived the Unit Block as a facing material. Two adjacent beveled squares were joined to form a **T** whose stem bonded into the body of the wall. One preliminary scheme used rough-laid stone masonry for major walls. As befits a semi-public residence, the house has large, open spaces and a generous entry that steps down to the living room. In some respects this spaciousness recalls the governor's mansion project of 1946. An eighteen-inch steel wide flange carries the roof over the large, glass-enclosed living room. The ribbed metal roof, beveled blocks, and ornamental doors with patterns of diamonds and squares complete a set of rich textural contrasts familiar in this architect's work. However, the large spaces here tend to vitiate the impact of the surfaces.

Another Chrysler executive, Lynn A. Townsend, chairman of the auto company, asked Dow for an elaborate house in 1963. The general massing of the house on its hill-side location (Fig. 113) is similar to the earlier proposal for another Chrysler man, K. T. Keller, in 1938.

Dow's early interest in low-cost housing was continued in a 1951–53 project for housing in Midland, for which 376 units were projected. Dow also provided designs for the Seafrontier Compound of the United States Embassy in the Philippines in 1956. The Sandwich House, whose construction system was explored in 1946, was finally built in 1952. The construction panels of Styrofoam core glued to plywood facings were developed in conjunction with a Dow Chemical product engineer in the summer of 1950. They were constructed on a fourteen-inch module for walls and roofs which were laid out in a three-foot-six-inch unit system.

A large number of college and community buildings came through the Dow office in the fifties and sixties. The Grace Dow Memorial Library, drawn in 1953, is a secular application of the brick walls, piers, and broad fascia first seen in the First Methodist Church in Midland several years earlier. In 1956, the city of Ann Arbor built a library very much in the same vein, with panels enameled in blue-green porcelain for its fascia.

Hillsdale College in southern Michigan, a conservative school stressing traditional American values, was the first college to commission buildings from Dow's office. As with subsequent jobs of this sort, the office tried to establish a continuing relationship with the institution which would result in future commissions as it grew, commissions often helped along by financial contributions from Midland people. For Delta College, Dow, along with the firm of Brysslebout and Wigen, built a large, multifunctional complex focused on a beautifully landscaped court (Fig. 114). Dow laid out Northwood Institute in Midland in 1962 and has added new buildings regularly since then. One of the buildings he proposed was a Creative Discussion School where two wings of radially organized discussion rooms were centered on a "control desk," presumably to ensure that the talk was creative. The Griswold Communications Center of 1971, built on a circular theme, was the final result. The Automotive Organization Team Hall of Fame of 1973 is a nave–side-aisle building whose large front doors open onto a display area. He also established a continuing relationship in 1960 with Interlochen Music Camp and Fine Arts School. Various classroom, dormitory, and performance structures were built in the pine woods of the northern lower peninsula. Facilities for Saginaw Valley, Muskegon, and Kalamazoo community colleges were designed in the middle and late sixties with the by now standard approach using brick and stucco.

Dow also designed Ann Arbor's striking city hall in 1961. The stucco and glass bands stepping out slightly at each higher level create an unusual form whose civic function is not immediately evident (Fig. 115). For the Livonia, Michigan, city hall, Dow proposed floors that advanced and receded in an irregular manner. Although it was never built, the proposal gave a larger, vertical building some picturesque irregularity.

The University of Michigan's administration building of 1966 (Fig. 116) is another

111

attempt to "compose" the surface of a large, blocky building. Its brick curtain wall fastened to the concrete structure is divided by what Dow called "cut stone tracery," which runs in irregularly spaced bands horizontally and vertically. Between the various squares and rectangles thus formed, windows are inserted, some in eighteen-inch bands at the ceilings of the rooms inside, some at the floor. Although as built the tracery is laid over brick, the original proposals had windows and colored squares and rectangles in a white stucco surface, recalling Dow's compositional patterns for stained glass and fabrics. In the same year, Wayne State University commissioned a design for a student center. Its top stories are covered in plaster divided into panels by bands and an irregular window arrangement. It seems that Dow's composition of contrasts is more effective in smaller buildings, where, because of their very size, the contrasts can be controlled; extending it to larger, repetitive structures, however, poses certain difficulties.

Alden Dow had had an abiding interest in theater design. As early as 1936 he was a subscriber to *Theater Arts* magazine. The first large auditorium he designed was in the 36th Division Memorial Competition, where a fairly conventional relationship of stage to seating was used. His next theater project was the Phoenix Civic Center five years later. There for the first time Dow used a side stage or runway opening off the front of the stage to enable the performance to spread out on either side of the audience as well as in front. The Grace Dow Library has a similar arrangement behind a row of brick piers. In the Northeast Intermediate School, also in Midland, the auditorium has similar side stages. The Henry McMorran Memorial Auditorium in Port Huron, Michigan, designed in 1957, has two side stages flanking a stage curtain of colored geometric overlays stitched onto a white background.

Eugene Power of Ann Arbor offered to give the University of Michigan a large theater for stage productions, and in 1964 Dow designed a large brick volume very similar to the later Midland Center for the Arts. The staging consultant for the university project was Jo Mielziner, who found that he could not go along with Dow's unusual proposals for the theater arrangement. A standoff resulted, and the university ended by hiring Roche and Dinkeloo as architects to work with Mielziner.

Four years later Dow got his chance to build the theater he had dreamed about for Midland (Figs. 117–18). The Midland Center for the Arts has an auditorium and a theater. The auditorium has long runways overlooking the audience. In this case, they are not directly accessible from the stage. The theater is a unique space whose great height stretches from above the revolving stage, closed off from the audience by folding panels, to the back of the seating area. In this great height run two levels of motorized light bridges, whose use still baffles directors who use the theater.

Notes

1. Personal communication, Robert G. Bell to the author, Traverse City, Michigan, July 30, 1980.

2. Letter of Frederick Graham to the author, March 5, 1970.

3. Office ledgers, Alden B. Dow Associates.

4. Quoted in *Midland Republican*, November 12, 1936, p. 4.

5. *Midland Republican*, December 24, 1936, p. 4, November 8, 1937, p. 6.

6. Personal communication, Robert G. Bell to the author, Traverse City, Michigan, July 30, 1980.

7. For a discussion of these churches, see Martin E. Marty, "The Architecture of Growth: The Five Dow-Designed Churches of Midland, Michigan," *Christian Century*, March 27, 1957, pp. 390–94.

8. Reported in *Architectural Record*, September, 1956, pp. 217–24; *House and Home*, November, 1956, pp. 156–59.

9. *House Beautiful*, June, 1962, pp. 90–95.

10. Curtis Besinger, "A House Built for Children to Enjoy and Remember," *House Beautiful*, August, 1962, pp. 82–87.

Architectural Work after 1950 / ILLUSTRATIONS

Work after 1950

Civic Center, Phoenix, Arizona, 1949, 1954, 1964. At the heart of the block-sized complex is a court with a pool and plants. Columns of pre-cast concrete and window areas contrast with stucco walls.

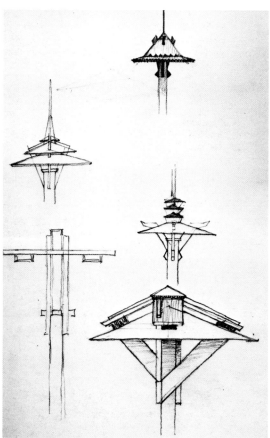

Lantern and beach house studies. These sketches show the correlation of visual images with geometric order and the way in which a single method of design can be applied to buildings and to the things that fit into those buildings.

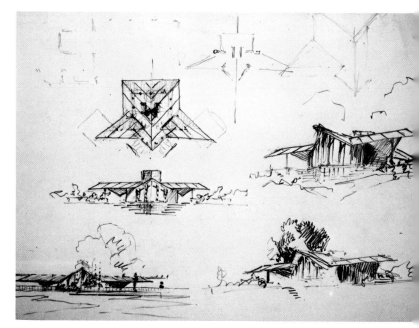

100   101

102

St. John's Episcopal Church, Midland, 1950. The nave of this church overlooks an enclosed garden on the street side. Dow first used church designs incorporating angled walls and roof in a project for Freeport, Texas, in 1943.

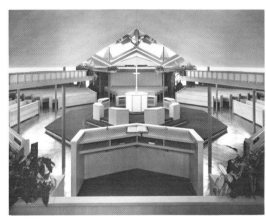

105

St. John's Lutheran Church, Midland, 1953. The centralized form focuses on the altar. Classrooms encircle the sanctuary, which is lighted from windows between two roofs.

104

Work after 1950

Christ Episcopal Church, Adrian, 1959. The asymmetrical composition of the elevation recalls Dow's earliest studies for his studio. The nave opens onto a landscaped courtyard.

106

108

an Reicker house, Midland, 1961. An intricate roof structure of
red joists on three levels tied together by short red posts con-
sts with planar brick walls and window areas. The large table
d ceiling lights in the centrally located living room repeat the
nstructional pattern. The angular, vertical lanterns (Fig. 109)
ovide an effective counterpoint to predominantly horizontal
mpositions.

109

110

111

*Mrs. Josephine Ashmun house, Midland, 1951. At the lower edges of the **A**-frame roof, Dow introduces glass and screens to make a simple geometry both useful and beautiful.*

Lynn Townsend house, Bloomfield Township, 1963. The outward tilt of the metal fascia distinguishes this large house from a project for another Chrysler executive twenty-five years earlier (Fig. 76). The interior walls of padded fabric mosaic emphasize the orthogonal geometry of the architecture.

113

Roscommon Congregational Church, Roscommon, 1961. An asymmetrical gable is prolonged as a spire in this direct expression of wood construction.

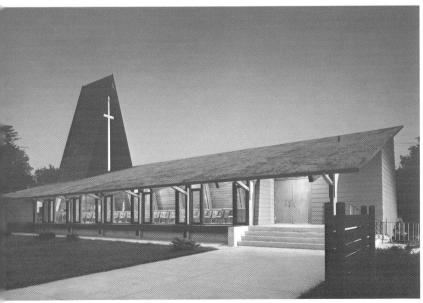

112

Work after 1950

Delta College, University Center, 1961. This landscaped court, whose plant forms and colors contrast with gently curved and rectangular pools, creates a picturesque view from surrounding windows.

114

115

City hall, Ann Arbor, 1961. Unbroken brick volumes contrasted with repeated textures of window bands are enlarged to fit a large civic structure.

University of Michigan administration building, Ann Arbor 1966. The repetitiveness of a seven-story office building camouflaged by geometric window and wall areas divided stone bands.

116

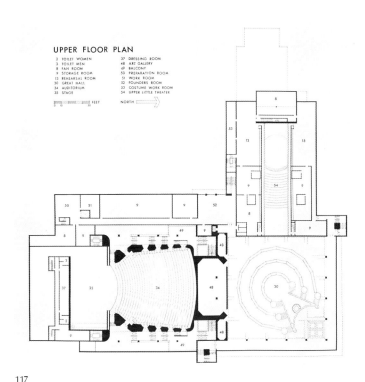

2 TOILET WOMEN   37 DRESSING ROOM
3 TOILET MEN   48 ART GALLERY
8 FAN ROOM   49 BALCONY
9 STORAGE ROOM   50 PREPARATION ROOM
13 REHEARSAL ROOM   51 WORK ROOM
30 GREAT HALL   52 FOUNDERS ROOM
34 AUDITORIUM   53 COSTUME WORK ROOM
35 STAGE   54 UPPER LITTLE THEATER

0 10   30 FEET   NORTH ⟹

...enter for the Arts, Midland, 1968. Dow's ideas about theater design and ...e importance of understanding one's own locale are reflected in this large ...vic structure, which restates on a much larger scale an architectural com-...osition used on earlier small buildings.

117

7. Design in the Community

If the more personal buildings of Alden Dow display a greater sense of completion than the larger public structures, Dow was not unaware of an even larger scale of design as well: community planning. Few architects have the opportunity to affect a whole community by their designs, but Dow has affected the built environment of Midland, Michigan, through numerous community structures, commercial establishments, and over seventy homes. From 1930 to the present he has been adding to the visual quality of the town, as it grew from eight thousand to over forty thousand inhabitants, and the unique result will be examined shortly.

A more concentrated opportunity for Dow to engage in community design, as noted earlier, began in 1941 in Lake Jackson, Texas. In the space of five years, Dow laid out the streets and designed housing and community structures for this new town on the Gulf Coast. Dow Chemical was expanding its plant in Freeport and the new town was to be built nearby for its employees (Fig. 119). As described in *Architecture and Design*, it was to be "a town composed in a southern jungle where the automobile and airplane are recognized necessities, and where zoning, public parks, individuality in streets and sites give insured residential values."[1] The curved streets "give infinite variety in character of building sites. Homeowners are offered all freedom possible in the use of their lot so long as it does not interfere with their neighbor."[2]

The street layout of the town is a delightful exercise in free-form curves tightly organized within and adjacent to the shopping center, in which the "buildings themselves form an integral part of a vast garden of shrubs, trees and flowers," according to a Lake Jackson company pamphlet. The plan falls squarely in the American tradition begun in Llewelyn Park in New Jersey by A. J. Davis[3] and in Riverside, Illinois, by Frederick Law Olmsted. More such broadly meandering streets were projected among the larger home sites to the north and west of the commercial center. The major streets are bounded by broad parkways, and a sequence of parks interlaces the denser residential areas near the town center. Immediately to the west of the town center is a prominent airport. The plan envisioned a town of five thousand acres, some three and a half miles long and a mile wide, with 2,800 inhabitants in 483 private homes and 100 government-built duplexes. About half the original plan was actually built.

Dow's sense of fun is evident not only in the playful street alignments but in their names, which, in addition to flower and tree names, include "This Way" and "That Way" streets in the shopping district (Fig. 120). For this town center Dow designed covered-sidewalk commercial structures. His own office was housed in a building with sloping sides forming the end of a line of stores. In this near-tropical setting, Dow employed a brilliant interior color scheme of blue-gray walls, bright green ceiling, magenta doors and trim, and the remaining surfaces in yellow. He also delighted in using the abundant large-leafed tropical plants as foils for the buildings. The movie house, schools, and churches were designed by Dow in his Houston office. Some schools in the surrounding county were also designed at this time.

Time has not been kind to Lake Jackson. Wartime restrictions required simple wooden buildings which have not stood up well in the humid conditions. The town center is barely holding its own in the face of shopping malls. The duplex housing has suffered particularly because of its minimal initial construction. The parkways are adequately maintained, but the parks near the commercial center are unkempt.

In neighboring Freeport, Dow designed some fifty houses as variations on two- and three-bedroom types. The first of these, drawn in Midland in March of 1940, was a thirty-three-foot-square, three-bedroom, low-pitched house in stucco. Variations were introduced by garages, maid's rooms, projected window bands, and porches. In the same year Dow designed a hotel and apartment buildings for Dow Chemical, a hospital, and a primary school. The Freeport houses have been well maintained in the last forty years and are still pleasant habitations among the foliage that was planted soon after construction.

Midland presents a very different countenance. Over a period of fifty years Dow has added buildings to a town largely dependent on the chemical company, buildings which grew from an older pattern and in response to an array of community forces. The Herbert Dow family was the pre-eminent family in town. Their large, picturesque house, "The Pines," on Main Street and Herbert Dow's Cadillac announced their position. When Dow returned to Midland from Wisconsin in 1933, he took his place in the cultural and social life of the town. His wife, Vada, was active in the Midland nursery and directed its Christmas toy exhibits for several years. These exhibits were held in Dow's studio, and the 1937 show featured a "doll house in the modern manner,"[4] with red floor, emerald green roof, and white walls.

After 1930 the center of Midland society became the country club. The Midland Guild presented its lecture series in the ballroom there. In 1934 Guild speakers included the historian Will Durant and the Mayan explorer Colonel Edward H. Thompson; in 1935 the choreographer Ruth St. Denis, the writer Maurice Hindus (who spoke on Soviet Russia), Ted Shawn and his company, the grand old actor Otis Skinner, Edward Weeks of the *Atlantic*, and John Goss and his "London Singers"; in other years the artist Rockwell Kent, the violinist Georges Enesco, and Reinhold Niebuhr (whose topic was "Does History Have a Meaning?").[5] Some special quality in this small Midwestern town is indicated by such a list of visitors.

The Dows were often guests at luncheons given at the country club by people who would later ask Dow to design houses for them. The Dows occasionally traveled with these acquaintances and joined them in the fun at costume parties. Various women's groups got together to discuss cultural matters; when the American Association of University Women were discussing fine arts, it invited Dow to talk on interior design or show his film relating buildings to nature's designs. The Monday Club, which discussed literature, invited Dow to talk to them about modern architecture.

The single focus of a company town gave continuing support to an architect who was an integral part of the community and who felt comfortable concentrating his work in his own back yard. Midland offered him a range of building types, from houses to scientific laboratories. The Midland paper often published photographs of the new buildings—from a garage for Oviatt's Bakery to houses, Dow Chemical offices, and other structures. The result for the town itself is a special case of local vernacular: in Midland, architecture is not represented by one or two showpieces but by a tradition based on Dow's designs. Architects who worked in Dow's studio and then left to continue on their own have extended the tradition.

Dow began his architectural practice by explaining his architecture to potential clients, pursued his career by building for them, and continued the contact afterward through friendships. A sense of sharing developed between designer and client that is rare. Most architects must draw commissions from a far larger, impersonal community which precludes the continuous contact that Dow enjoyed in Midland. The lasting effect on the people of Midland, of course, is hard to determine.

The Dow Foundation has added a significant complex of community facilities across the road from the Midland Country Club and back of Alden Dow's house. The Midland Cultural Center began with the Grace A. Dow Memorial Library, designed in 1953 (Figs. 121–22). The basic space, containing book stacks, reading room, and small theater, is extended by rows of square brick piers carrying heavy, paneled fascia made of finely crushed bottle glass. When the Midland Center for the Arts was completed in 1970, its high mansard roofs of ribbed metal suggested a coordination with the library through color, so the library fascia was changed to ribbed metal panels painted to match the larger building.

Midland is a long way from company town experiments like Port Sunlight outside of Liverpool, not only in distance but in a freedom from explicit patronage which is reflected in its physical appearance. There is, however, a pervasive ideal there being held up for emulation by the community.

Notes

1. *Architecture and Design*, June, 1943.

2. Brush-lettered sign in the Alden B. Dow Associates archives.

3. On Llewellyn Park, see Richard Guy Wilson, "Idealism and the Origin of the First American Suburb: Llewellyn Park, New Jersey," *American Art Journal*, October, 1979, pp. 79–90.

4. *Midland Republican*, November 11, 1937, p. 6.

5. *Midland Republican*, March 1, April 12, 1934, January 31, October 14, November 11, 1935, January 28, February 16, May 14, 1937.

Design in the Community / ILLUSTRATIONS

119

Lake Jackson, Texas, 1942. This company tow laid out on the Gulf Coast near the Dow Chemic installations used a curvilinear street pattern ar distinct neighborhoods to achieve a strong visu and social order.

Park restrooms, Lake Jackson, Texas, 1944. This small structure shows how formal inventiveness can turn a necessity into a diverting whimsy.

120

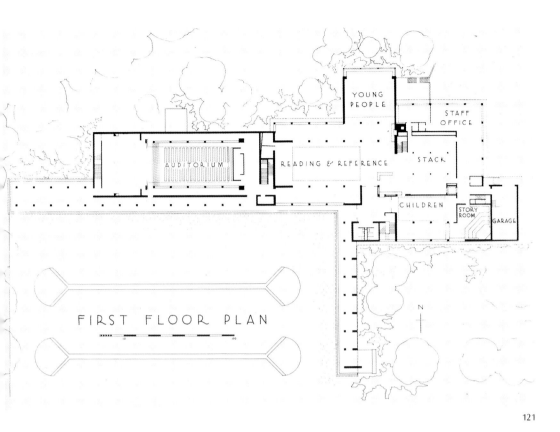

FIRST FLOOR PLAN

YOUNG PEOPLE

STAFF OFFICE

AUDITORIUM

READING & REFERENCE

STACK

CHILDREN

STORY ROOM

GARAGE

N

121

Grace A. Dow Memorial Library, Midland, 1953. Lines of brick columns passing in front of and beyond smooth brick walls create an extended plan and textural contrast. An open central space gives a living-room feeling to a multi-functional building.

122

8. An Architecture and a Life

The most effective demonstration of the connection between architecture and life is Dow's own house-studio and life. In some respects his architecture is satisfying in proportion to its similarity to his own home and the life lived therein. Dow's house was added to the studio in 1940 (Fig. 123). The designs of 1939 show a less playful building than the studio. Its roofs are flat or hipped forms covered by ribbed copper. Generous expanses of carpeted space are substituted for the smaller, livelier spaces in the studio.

While the earliest part of the studio was built simply with wooden structural members, the house is supported on a considerable array of steel beams, columns, and joists. The entrance to the studio is on the lower level, through Dow's study which is at the end of the long studio drafting room. The large porch off the dining room is screened from floor to cantilevered roof, which affords an unbroken vista from corner to corner. The view from this broad expanse overlooks the enlarged stream edged in pines, willows, and other trees and shrubbery chosen for their textures and colors.

Dow's house became the setting for his own explorations of color and composition, which often served as models for details of other buildings. He provided continuous embellishment for his own architectural framework, which itself has not changed significantly since the house was first built. For example, on the floor of the playroom beneath his living room, he created a colorful composition of linoleum arranged in circles, bars, and squares that related to the semicircular seating before the fireplace and to the small stage area. Recently he has replaced that hard surface with a hard-nap carpeting which copies the original composition. Above the stairs leading to the playroom is a hanging sculpture of colored discs and squares. The Midland Country Club lounge and the Arbury playroom preceded Dow's use in his own house of ornamental colors and shapes on ceilings, floors, and walls (Figs. 124–25).

Other patterns of geometry and color appear in various textile embellishments of his buildings. The curtains in the McMorran Auditorium and the auditorium of the Midland Center for the Arts. (Fig. 126) are the largest-scale examples of this compositional contrast. They were made in an applique technique. In stained glass, Dow's patterns appear at their most elaborate in the First Methodist Church. The chapel is a simple, high space in which the seating is balanced between a plain brick wall and a full-height glass wall divided by his modular, orthogonal geometry (Fig. 127). Another chapel, this one for the Dearborn Presbyterian Church, elaborates a triangular geometry through its plan and its richly textured wall, constructed of structural concrete blocks laid in angled beds and pierced with triangular bits of glass. At a certain scale these patterns take on the fascination of puzzles. It was necessary to elaborate and intensify the patterns inherent in the architecture itself as the size of the building increased: at a certain point the small-scale expression of constructional pattern had to be dropped entirely. These areas of pattern were introduced to re-establish a balanced contrast with the building. Dow's use of this kind of pattern is usually very successful, but even he acknowledges that the story-high band of ornament on the Center for the Arts in Midland is not successfully related to the structure as a whole. The ornament remains unfinished to this day.

Dow looks upon collecting things as a particularly appropriate expression for an individual exercising his power of appreciation and discrimination. For example, from very early childhood he has been fascinated by railroads, running to photograph a 1923 wreck on the Pere Marquette line, which ran in front of his home. Model trains run above the sitting room of the bedroom suite and in the basement of his house. Dow shared with Bob Goodall this love of railroading. He appreciates the model engines not only for their engineering but for their composition of shapes and parts, a kind of mechanistic model of design that complements his interest in nature as a model.

The arts are represented by a collection of sculptures in both a modernized classical form of the twenties and in the work of Marshall Fredericks. Beside the elevated dining hearth stand Fredericks' small bronze figures called "Saints and Sinners," a range of medieval personalities including a knight, a lady, and a devil. The crafts are represented by a collection of pottery distributed throughout the living room and bedrooms. Beautiful jars and vases provide the proper contrast of vivid colors and flowing forms with the rectilinear modularity of the interiors (Fig. 128).

The camera has provided Dow with a most effective tool for revealing the world of composition as he sees it. He has worked with still and moving pictures from his youth. On a trip to Europe with his family early in 1926, he took movies of the sights, including views from the crow's nest on the ship, from the Eiffel Tower, and from the airplane on the flight from Paris to London. He also took many still and moving pictures on his trip with his Columbia classmates three years later. When he and his wife travel today, he continues to take his cameras, as he believes that the camera is a great tool for composing views that balance contrasts of visual elements.

In 1954 at the Grace Dow Memorial Library, Dow staged the first performance of "Somnaphonics."[1] Movement, color, and music were integrated into a new art form, as dancers' shadows from colored lights were cast on a translucent plastic screen (provided by Dow Chemical), the lights coordinated with the piano music of Debussy, Scriabin, and others.

Dow was involved with landscape gardening from his boyhood, as he watched and assisted his father in making their three-acre backyard into thirty-acre garden. He also continued his father's cultivation of orchids. His first executed design was a concrete bridge (now destroyed) built for his brother in 1927 (Fig. 129). In succeeding years he added various whimsies that enabled one to cross the stream flowing through the Dow gardens. On the boat to Japan in 1923 the Dow family met Paul Takuma Tono, who was returning to Waseda University in Tokyo after receiving a master's degree in landscape design from Cornell. Herbert Dow invited him to come to Midland to help the town with its gardens. On May 1, 1925, Tono arrived for a three-month stay, during which he worked on a rock garden at the city park and served as judge for the prize money awarded each month to the best gardens in town. The August flower show included a rock garden put together by Tono, Alden's oldest brother Willard, and the Dow gardens gardener, Elzie Cote. The ingredients were a pool, pines, rocks, ferns, and moss.

Alden Dow most often uses landscape design to contrast natural forms with the hard-edged forms of buildings. The context he most often imagines for his buildings is a landscape setting, not a continuous urban environment. The contrast of structure and planting was employed in the first building Dow designed, the Midland Country Club of 1930. The great importance of the planting in "securing the intended effect with the exceedingly plain lines of the modern cream stucco building" was faithfully described in the *Midland Republican*.[2] To the south of the clubhouse a grass slope linked the entrance level with the locker room level. This area, called a "cube garden," played off the irregularity of plants and grass with squared-off concrete.

In 1972 Dow returned to his father's garden and began a major program of renovation. The once free-flowing stream, now near stagnation, was made part of a closed system driven by a pump. A rocky waterfall camouflages this artifical system, whose eight-inch pipe spills into a new rill cut through the lawn, completing the circuit with the original stream. Several new bridges of concrete and steel (Fig. 130) were added or replaced older ones. Dow also made use of a principle of spatial manipulation in landscape learned from his father: an area of lawn can be made to appear larger if it is bowl-shaped, with the corners higher than the center. Dow's earth-shaping in the garden resulted in a playful area called "Ups and Downs" (Fig. 131).

Dow revealed his perpetual sense of wonder to me one morning in 1975, as we stood in front of the studio. He looked about to see if anyone was around, then beckoned me through the curtain of trailing branches of the mulberry tree nearby. His upward glance directed my attention to the marvelously arched enclosure filtering the soft, green light. He remarked, as he looked round, that he had tried to capture this narrow space in a photograph. Later in the day, while staking out locations for trees at the Midland Art Center, he spied a similarly trailing apple tree and almost imperceptibly nodded to me, to mark another extraordinary space.

On one lovely summer's evening, Dow and I stepped onto the elevated porch overlooking his stream and garden. A few birds were singing; we could see fish in the water below. The stone lantern he brought back from Japan twenty years before stood on its little "beach." Everything seemed arranged to perfection. But as he looked out Dow said, "It's lonely here. I did not set out to make it this way, but it's like the Englishman looking out of his house and seeing nothing that isn't his."[3] He had, after all, been looking out on this view for nearly forty years. The excitement of first arranging this composition of contrasts can be immediately re-created by any visitor, but after living in it for years different concerns arise. A place that surrounds one's whole life may be satisfying to begin with, but its carefully arranged balance may need to be revitalized. Dow acknowledged the effect of time on sensory experience in a talk to the Monday Club many years earlier: "Everyone knows that he cannot eat cornflakes for every meal and continue to like them and in the same way."[4]

These comments on his own house forty years after it was built suggest a remarkable fidelity to basic ideals even as their paradoxes were uncovered. The ideal of composure could hardly be embodied more convincingly. It also seems appropriate that the realization of the transiency of stillness, like the momentary mirror of the pond, should produce a kind of sadness, though neither Dow nor the eighteenth-century proponent of the Picturesque Richard Payne Knight would succumb to sentimentality. From its earliest formulation, however, Picturesque theory sought to escape the limitations of design based on the transitory sensory impact of surprise; Knight concocted the notion of "permanent novelty" to this end.[5]

Dow has recently returned, as if for consolation, to a parable by Lafcadio Hearn that he had read years earlier at the urging of a Columbia classmate. "Readings in a Dream Book" is a moving dialogue between a wave and the sea. The wave fears the loss of individuality; the sea comforts it by saying that it will not be lost, that a return to the sea is part of an eternal cycle in a great "Rhythm of Life." "There is no rest in me," the sea repeats.[6] Dow now says that this is the most important thing that he has read.

Alden Dow stands loyally within a tradition that he was able to carry forward virtually without compromise. Some of these ideals can be completely realized only in the most favorable social and economic circumstances. The primacy of the individual, whether as citizen, homeowner, or self-reliant judge of aesthetic experience, is enshrined in the American tradition. The Picturesque aesthetic grew out of the very late eighteenth-century principles on which this republic was founded. The notion of the private house as "architecture" developed in the nineteenth century in this country along with other uniquely American institutions and beliefs. The danger of isolation was present in the American tradition from the beginning. When the wilderness ceased to be a physical place, it was to be remade by individual poets according to a myth of nature. For example, Edgar Allen Poe's poetic theory was based on a marriage of science and art in the service of sensory effect. His story "The Domain of Arnheim" is a report by a visitor to a magical landscape garden. In the story a gentleman possessing money, opportunity, and taste combined them to create a beautiful, isolated place. There is no report from the creator of the garden, but taking up residence in such an interior world could lead to an end like that of Roderick Usher. Dow's insight regarding loneliness saves him from that fate.

The lack of strain, the sense of composure, that one feels in Dow's studio results from the complete harmony of the ideals and the means of achieving them. As he read Emerson's essay on "Experience," Dow marked a passage that suggests he made his choice of means and ends very consciously: "There is no adaptation or universal applicability in men, but each has his special talent, and the mastery of successful men consists in adroitly keeping themselves where and when that turn shall be oftenest practiced."[7] Alden Dow's architecture demonstrates the power and beauty of composition as well as its limitations. It is applicable at the scale immediately perceptible to the individual and at the invisible scale of ethical diagrams, but the middle range of communal life is left unresolved. When the angle of our vision takes in only the successful composition, we can appreciate the intentional balance of contrasts. From a larger angle, our vision takes in elements in conflict with the composed order of the smaller view. This uncomposed contrast engages our own imaginations to search for a new harmony or to wonder about the very nature of harmony itself.

Notes

1. "Somnaphonics" is described in Elaine Plummer and Jean Stark, "A Picture Painted in Sound," *Etude*, September, 1956, pp. 15, 50.

2. *Midland Republican*, May 30, 1931, p. 4.

3. Interview of July, 1979.

4. Quoted in *Midland Republican*, April 25, 1935, p. 2.

5. Richard Payne Knight, *An Analytical Inquiry into the Principles of Taste* (Hants, England, 1972), p. 448.

6. Lafcadio Hearn, "The Wave," in *Shadowing and a Japanese Miscellany*, vol. 10 of *The Writings of Lafcadio Hearn* (Boston, 1922), pp. 174–76.

7. Emerson, *Essays*, 2d ser., p. 60.

An Architecture and a Life / ILLUSTRATIONS

Alden Dow house, Midland, 1939–40. The residence portion of the studio complex is raised a story above the pond. A desire for comfort and privacy resulted in a generous living room (Fig. 123) whose ceiling is of woven plastic strips, glowing from concealed lights.

123

Compare the playroom of the And son Arbury house in Midland of 19 (Fig. 124) with the lounge of the M land Country Club of 1937 (Fig. 12 Dow intensified the geometry of architecture by introducing areas small-scale patterns of color to co trast with adjacent plane surfaces wall and ceiling: in the playroom, li leum, paint, and light bulbs: in lounge, a painted mural that cont ued up onto the ceiling.

124

...nter for the Arts, Midland, 1968, auditorium. The pat-
...n appliquéd on the stage curtain is a concentrated
...ea of color and geometry in a large hall with red car-
...t, green upholstery, and white walls.

126

125

The large geometric window wall of the First Methodist Church chapel (Fig. 127) of 1952 is balanced by the metal gate at the other end of the courtyard. Compare the living room of the Dow house (Fig. 128), where every corner of the composition demonstrates the balance of textures, and arrangements are easily changed to allow further refinements.

127

Dow gardens, Midland, 1927. This concrete bridge, built 1927, was Dow's first design.

128

129

This bridge in the Dow gardens, built fifty years after the one shown in Figure 129, is faithful to the same aesthetic principle: red metal contrasts with green foliage and geometry contrasts with nature.

...is rolling lawn in the Dow gardens, created in 1977, of-
...s a visual contrast with its surroundings as well as pro-
...ding the opportunity to have fun running up and
...wn.

131

Bibliography

Although Alden Dow did not solicit publication in the magazines, he had received notable exposure in the professional press since 1936. In September of that year, *Architectural Forum* introduced Dow to its readers in a nine-page review of his earliest work. *Forum* noted his place in the Wrightian tradition while recognizing his own individuality. In December the magazine featured the Heath house. Dow was represented, along with Royal Barry Wills, Hugh Stubbins, Rudolph M. Schindler, H. H. Harris, Richard Neutra, John Lloyd Wright, and W. W. Wurster, in a selection of fifty new houses in the April, 1937, issue. In 1939 *Forum* published the MacCallum house and *Architectural Record* presented the Diehl and Mary Dow houses.

In a review of the "40 under 40" show at the Architectural League in the April, 1941, issue of *Forum*, Talbot Hamlin looked approvingly at those designs which exhibited the clear and simple elegance of Edward D. Stone's Goodyear house, but he was made uncomfortable by the "overelaborate eccentricities of Alden Dow's jagged office roof." The Campbell house is the only Dow work illustrated in the review, and its calm domesticity cannot fairly be characterized as "fantastic," to use Hamlin's word. *Pencil Points* devoted seventeen pages in its May, 1942, issue to a comprehensive review of Dow's work and thoughts, including plans and photographs. Hamlin was called upon to write the accompanying essay. Though he placed Dow squarely in the Wright camp, he responded most enthusiastically to those houses which diverge in their simplicity from the textural richness identified with Wright. In general, Hamlin tended to be grudging in his presentation, although the editors gave Dow a voice by quoting at some length from a letter he had sent them explaining his buildings.

The Texas projects at Freeport and Lake Jackson and the Midland Hospital received due notice in the press during the war. The most singular presentation however, was in the June, 1943, issue of *Architecture and Design*, published by the Architectural Catalog Company in New York, which devoted the whole issue to Dow, using his own layout. George Nelson and Henry Wright included two interiors by Dow in their 1945 book *Tomorrow's House*, in which most architects included came from California, Illinois, Massachusetts, or New York.

In the May, 1945, *Architectural Record*, Dow's former history teacher at Columbia, Joseph Hudnut, illustrated his essay on the "post-modern" house with a photograph of the Saunders commission. The essay recommended the humanization of the engineering, scientific, and intellectual aspects of modern houses through emotional content, but it is not clear whether the houses Hudnut shows illustrate the problem or the solution! Hudnut also illustrates (without identification) the work of Van Evera Bailey, Richard Neutra, George Fred Keck, Gregory Ain with George Agron, and Royal Barry Wills, and closes with the reminder, "Houses will still be built out of human hearts."

Bibliography

In addition to the professional coverage, Dow was featured in two issues of *Life*. An article on the current state of housing in the United States in November, 1937, devoted three pages to Midland and Dow's houses, including the $2,500 Lewis house and the $50,000 Pardee house. Twelve years later, as we have seen, *Life* returned to Midland and Dow's work.

1932   *Architectural Record.* June, pp. 394–400.
Midland Country Club

1936   *Architectural Forum.* September, pp. 191–200.
Stein, Whitman, Cavanagh, and Diehl houses; Dow studio.

Architectural Forum. December, pp. 524–525.
Heath house.

1937   "50 New Houses." *Architectural Forum.* April, pp. 354–355.
Hanson house.

"Midland, Michigan Leads the Way in Private Housing." *Life,* November 15, pp. 50–52.

1939   *Architectural Record.* March, pp. 54–55, 63–64.
Diehl house.

Architectural Forum. April, pp. 278–279.
John Best house.

Architectural Forum. June, p. 490.
Dow Chemical Golden Gate Exposition exhibit.

"Modern House in America." *Architectural Forum.* July, pp. 60–62.
MacCallum house.

Architectural Record. August, p. 61.
Diehl house vanity.

Architectural Record. September, pp. 46–48, 58.
Mary Dow house.

Architectural Record. December, p. 53.
MacCallum house game room.

1940   "Plastics and Architecture." *Architectural Record.* July, pp. 62, 66–76.
Greene house bedroom; model of Dow Chemical plastic sheet house; Midland bath house; Dow Chemical Golden Gate Exposition exhibition.

House and Garden. December, p. 36.
Pardee House.

1941   *Architectural Record.* January, pp. 99–101.
Greene house.

Architectural Forum. March, pp. 189–191.
Pardee house.

Architectural Record. April, pp. 94–95.
Band shell and bath house, Midland.

Interiors. August, p. 48.
Pryor house living room.

Architectural Record. October, pp. 78–79.
Hodgkiss house.

1942   *Architectural Forum.* March, pp. 177–181.
Rood and Pryor houses.

Architectural Record. April, pp. 47, 62.
Freeport, TX, houses.

Talbot Hamlin. "The Architect and House." *Pencil Points.* May, pp. 269–286.
Saunders, Arbury, Hanson, Heath, Pardee, and Grant houses; Dow studio.

Architectural Record. May, p. 56.
Hotel, Freeport, TX

1943   Mary Ellen Green and Mark Murphy. "The Town a Test Tube Built." *Saturday Evening Post.* May 1, pp. 20–21, 97–98.

Architecture and Design. June issue.

Interiors. June, pp. 49–53.

1944   *Architectural Record.* January, pp. 67–68.
Hotel, Freeport, TX

Insured Mortgage Portfolio. First Quarter, pp. 11–13.
Lake Jackson, TX

Dow Diamond. May, pp. 1–14.
Lake Jackson, TX

M.S.A. *Weekly Bulletin.* November 14, p. 15.
Texas Memorial Competition winner.

Pencil Points. December, pp. 47–58.
Reorganized Church of Latter Day Saints, Midland.

1945   *Chemical Industries.* January, pp. 49–52.
Color on Dow Chemical Plant, Midland.

Alden B. Dow. "Color: The New Element in Industry."
Dow Diamond. February, pp. 15–18.

Architectural Forum. March, p. 82.

Architectural Forum. April.
Grant house in Owens Corning advertisement.

"Color in Balance." *Hospitals Magazine.* June.
Midland hospital.

Dow Diamond. June, pp. 4–5.
Dow Chemical St. Louis offices.

Pencil Points. August, pp. 56, 66.
Midland hospital.

"When Building Starts Again." *Motor News.* August.

George Nelson and Henry Wright. *Tomorrow's House.*
New York, pp. 5, 25.
Pryor house living room; Rood house living room.

"Acoustic of Music Shells." *Pencil Points.* September,
p. 97.
Midland band shell.

1946   *Architectural Forum.* February, pp. 92–93.
Ingersoll houses, Kalamazoo.

Interiors. May, pp. 86–87.
Ingersoll houses, Kalamazoo.

Architectural Forum. July, pp. 128–129.
John Best house.

1947   Maron J. Simon. *Your Solar House.* New York, pp.
66–67.
Michigan solar house.

M.S.A. *Weekly Bulletin.* February, p. 47.
Governor's mansion.

Alden B. Dow. "Planning the Contemporary House."
Architectural Record. November, pp. 89–95.
Irish house.

Architectural Forum. December, p. 104.
Ingersoll houses, Kalamazoo.

1948   "Architecture: Alden Dow." *Life.* March 15, pp. 88–92.

House and Garden. August, pp. 58–59.
Irish house.

Talbot Hamlin. "The Work of Alden B. Dow." *Nuestra
Arquitectura.* (Buenos Aires.) November, pp.
371–396.
Dow studio; MacCallum, Arbury, Hanson, Ball, Heath,
Mary Dow, MacMartin, Irish, Saunders, and Rood
houses; Reorganized Church of Latter Day Saints,
Midland.

1949   "Modern Houses . . . ." *Time.* August 15, p. 60.
Saxton house, Flint.

L'Architecture d'aujourd'hui. May, p. 14.
Music kiosk, Midland.

1951   *Journal of Royal Architectural Institute of Canada.*
July, pp. 202–208.
Reorganized Church of Latter Day Saints, Midland.

1952   *Better Building and Equipment.* April.
Northeast Intermediate School, Midland.

Architectural Forum. December, pp. 95–97.
First Methodist Church, Midland.

1953   *Detroit Free Press,* Roto Magazine. January 4.

M.S.A. *Monthly Bulletin.* February, pp. 17–43.

Architectural Record. December, p. 156.
Ashmun house.

1955   "The Architect and His Community." *Progressive Ar-
chitecture.* February, pp. 80–93.
Ashmun, Ballmer, and R. W. Bennett houses; First
Methodist Church, Midland; high school, Midland.

Detroit News, Pictorial Magazine. April 24.
Midland library.

Time. September 19, p. 80.
St. John's Lutheran Church.

Library Journal. December 1, pp. 2696–2704.
Midland and Phoenix libraries.

Architectural Forum. December, p. 142.
St. John's Lutheran Church.

M.S.A. *Monthly Bulletin.* December, pp. 20–21.
Grace A. Dow Library, Midland.

1956   *Brick and Tile.* January, pp. 1, 4–5.
Ashmun and Bennett houses.

Architectural Record. April, p. 11.
First Methodist Church, Midland.

"Color Is Catching On." *Chemical Week.* July 28,
p. 30.

Bibliography

Elaine Plummer and Jean Stark. "A Picture Painted in Sound." *Etude*. September, pp. 15, 50.

1957 *Church Management*. January.
First Methodist Church, Midland.

"Planning the Church Building." *Your Church*. February.
First Methodist Church, Midland.

"The Architecture of Growth: The Five Dow-Designed Churches of Midland." *Christian Century*. March 27, pp. 390–394.

Architectural Forum. April, pp. 122–125.
Grace A. Dow Library.

"Architecture Is for People." *Detroit Free Press*. Sunday Roto Living. October 27.

1958 M.S.A. *Monthly Bulletin*. p. 13.
St. John's Episcopal Church, Midland.

1959 Alden B. Dow. "An Architect's View of Creativity." *Creativity and Its Cultivation*. Edited by Harold H. Anderson. New York, pp. 30–43.

Alden B. Dow. "An Architect's View of Creativity." *Journal of the American Institute of Architects*. February, pp. 19–26.

"Your Legacy from Frank Lloyd Wright." *House Beautiful*. October, pp. 208–211, 230.
Alden B. Dow studio and house; Ashmun house.

Point West. December.
Phoenix Art Museum.

"Consider the A-Frame." *House Beautiful*. December, pp. 162–163.

1961 Alden B. Dow. "The Continuity of Idea and Form." *Four Great Makers of Modern Architecture*. New York, pp. 25–26.

"Profiles in Design—1." *House and Home*. February, pp. 110–123.

Lillian Jackson Brown. "A Natural House with a River View." *Detroit Free Press*, Sunday Roto Living. May 28.
James Duffy house.

1962 Ada Louise Huxtable. "Water: The Wine of Architecture." *Horizon*. May, pp. 30–31.
Alden B. Dow studio and house.

"Garden Lights Should Do More Than Light." *House Beautiful*. June, pp. 90–95.

Curtis Besinger. "How A Corporation President Built to Entertain Guests." *House Beautiful*. September, pp. 124–135, 207.
Leland I. Doan house.

Curtis Besinger. "A Home Built for Children to Enjoy and Remember." *House Beautiful*. August, pp. 82–87, 107.
Keeler house.

"Patterns in Thought—An Interview With Alden Dow, F.A.I.A." M.S.A. *Monthly Bulletin*. November.

1963 "Architect's Garden in the Midwest." *Continental*. May–June.

Architectural Record. July, pp. 136–139.
Christ Episcopal Church, Adrian.

Progressive Architecture. October, pp. 202–205.
Ann Arbor City Hall.

M.S.A. *Monthly Bulletin*.
Ann Arbor City Hall.

1965 "Alden Dow's Architect's Office and Home, Midland, Michigan." *Modern Architecture U.S.A.*, *Museum of Modern Art and the Graham Foundation for Advanced Studies in the Fine Arts*. Example 12.

1967 M.S.A. *Monthly Bulletin*. May.
Institute of Social Research, University of Michigan; Dearborn Presbyterian Church.

"He's Changed the Face of His World." *Detroit Free Press*. July.

"Five Buildings by Alden B. Dow." *Architectural Record*. September, pp. 165–176.
Kalamazoo nature center; First Presbyterian Church, Dearborn; Carras house; Y.W.C.A., Saginaw; Reicker house.

1970 Alden B. Dow. *Reflections*. Midland.

Project Drawings

Note: Where no location is given, the project is generic or the site is unknown. The list stops in 1967, when the volume of work increased to the point that Dow himself was not as close to each project as he had been in earlier years.

Asterisks indicate projects which were not built.

Year	Project	Location
1927	Bridge for Dow gardens	Midland
1930	Midland Country Club	Midland
1932	Towsley house	Ann Arbor
1933	Stein house	Midland
	Heatley house°	Midland
	Lewis house	Midland
1934	Cavanagh house	Midland
	Dow studio	Midland
	Heath house	Midland
	Hanson house	Midland
	Oviatt's garage	Midland
	US 10 shops°	Midland
	Willard Dow house addition	Midland
	Whitman house	Midland
1935	Dow studio	Midland
	Arbury cottage addition	Midland
	MacCallum house	Midland
	Ball house	Midland
	Frolic Theater remodeled	Midland
	Diehl house	Midland
	Mitts houses°	Saginaw
	Jonescue house°	Dearborn
	E. W. Bennett house addition	Midland
	Dubois house	Flint
	L. I. Doan house addition	Midland
	Low cost housing°	Midland
	Johnston cabin°	Lansing
	Dow Chemical main office remodeled, addition	Midland
1936	Pardee house	Midland
	Mary Dow house	Saginaw
	Greene house	Midland
	Dow Chemical clock room°	Midland
	Wyckoff house°	Mt. Pleasant
	E. W. Bennett cottage	Benmark
	Towsley cabin	Benmark
	Saunders house	Bloomfield Hills
	Dow studio	Midland
	Colignan house (A & B)°	Muskegon
	Apartment building°	Mt. Pleasant
	Panter house	Midland
	Conner house	Midland
1937	Bachman house	East Lansing
	School addition	Merrill
	Dow studio	Midland
	Pryor house	Grosse Pointe Park
	Bath house (municipal)	Midland
	Koerting house	Elkhart, IN
	Dow Chemical addition	Midland
	Presbyterian manse remodeled	Midland
	Barstow cottage addition	Ludington
	"1940" house°	
	W. F. Brown house	Mt. Pleasant
	Barclay house	Midland
	Dow Chemical main office addition	Midland
	Hotel°	Ann Arbor
	Dow Chemical organic laboratory°	Midland
	Band shell	Midland
	Nursery	Midland
1938	Keller house°	
	$3,000 house°	
	Cummings house°	Ypsilanti
	Dow Chemical exhibit	San Francisco, CA
	Carlson houses (2)°	
	Rood house	Kalamazoo
	Judson house°	Midland
	Solosky store°	Midland
	Wildes house	Midland
	Best house	Midland
	Ethyl Dow Chemical Company house°	Cape Fear, NC
1939	Hodgkiss house	Petoskey
	Sherk house alternatives°	Midland
	Brown Lumber Company	Midland
	Erickson house (A & B)°	
	Ingleside Housing°	Detroit
	Arbury house	Midland
	Fleming house	Elkhart, IN
	Morrison house	
	L. I. Doan beach house	Crystal Lake
	Campbell house	Midland
	Edick house addition°	
	A. B. Dow house	Midland
	Dow Chemical house "101"°	
1940	Wells house	Grosse Pointe
	Grant house	Midland
	Dow Chemical laboratory°	Ann Arbor
	Dowell exhibition building°	
	"Narrow Lot" house°	
	Dow Chemical offices	New York, RCA Building
	Dow Chemical hotel	Freeport, TX
	Dow Chemical apartments	Freeport, TX
	Garfield house addition°	Clare
	R. Brown clinic°	
	Towsley nursery°	Ann Arbor
	Dow Chemical houses	Freeport, TX

Project Drawings

	Driesbach house	Midland
	Hospital	Freeport, TX
	Rich house	Midland
	Dow Chemical laboratory	Midland
	Dow Chemical office	Freeport, TX
	School°	Barnett
	Smith house	Algonac
	Dow Chemical main office	Midland
	Dow Chemical office°	Seal Beach, CA
	Carr apartments°	Mt. Pleasant
	Olsen house°	Alton, IL
	Loose house°	Midland
	Rich Press Building	Midland
1941	Dow Chemical houses	Freeport, TX
	MacMartin house	Midland
	Short house°	Midland
	Irish house	Midland
	Reinke house	Midland
	Butenschoen house	Midland
	Bass house	Midland
	Boonstra house	Midland
	Carr house	Mt. Pleasant
	Grebe house	Midland
	Dow Chemical office°	Pittsburg, CA
	Robinson house	Grosse Pointe Park
	Low cost house°	
	Barstow house alteration	Midland
	Low cost houses°	
	Reorganized Church of Latter Day Saints	Midland
	Reed house°	Houston, TX
	MacMartin store°	Harbor Springs
	Dow Chemical office	Freeport, TX
	Penhaligan house	Midland
1942	Dow Chemical office addition°	Velasco, TX
	Parents' and Children's School	Midland
	Dow Chemical laboratory	Freeport, TX
	Primary school	Freeport, TX
	Midland Hospital	Midland
1943	Dow Chemical display booth	Houston, TX
	Salvation Army chapel	Midland
	Barnes Manufacturing office remodeled	Mansfield, OH
	Federal Work Agency attached houses	Brazoria, TX
	Dow Corning service buildings	Midland
	Lutheran church°	Freeport, TX
	Circle house°	
	Service Hospital°	Texas
	Town plan	Lake Jackson, TX
1944	Midland Hospital	Midland
	Lutheran church°	Midland
	Kreger house°	Grosse Ile
	Dow Chemical offices	St. Louis, MO

	Donnell house°	Findlay, OH
	36th Army Division Memorial building°	Texas
	U. S. Plywood house°	
1945	Burdick house°	Midland
	Baptist church°	Sweeny, TX
	Methodist church°	Lake Jackson, TX
	American Legion clubhouse°	Grayling
	Dow Chemical laboratory	Midland
	Knepp's store°	Midland
	Maher house addition°	
	Draper house°	Houston, TX
	Ingersoll Steel houses	Kalamazoo
	O'Koomian house°	
	Sandwich panels°	
	Hanchett house°	Big Rapids
	L-O-F Solar house°	
	Memorial chapel°	Midland
1946	Dowell laboratory°	Tulsa, OK
	Small House 100°	
	First Presbyterian Church°	Lake Jackson, TX
	Peloubet house°	Midland
	Tri-City Airport°	Saginaw
	Gardner house°	
	Dow Chemical plastics office°	Midland
	Property layout (housing)°	Houston, TX
	Sandwich refrigerator°	
	Governor's residence°	Lansing
	Detroit Edison display kitchen°	Detroit
	Dow Chemical auditorium°	Freeport, TX
	Charch house	Chadds Ford, PA
	Zass house°	Midland
	W. Bennett house°	Ludington
1947	Dow Corning offices	New York, Empire State Building
	National Bank	Midland
	Douma house°	Petoskey
	Kirk house	Midland
	First Methodist Church	Midland
	Heisman's store°	Midland
	Moutsatson store°	Midland
	Chemical Bank alteration	Midland
	Whiting house	Midland
	Burgess Music Store°	Midland
	Towns house alterations°	Midland
	Reorganized Church of Latter Day Saints°	Grand Rapids
	Roger's Beauty Studio°	Midland
	Church of the Nazarene°	
	Arbury house alterations°	Midland
	Saxton house	Flint
1948	Indian River Shrine°	
	Mode Motors°	Midland
	Wilson Funeral addition°	Midland

150

	Baptist parsonage°	Midland
	Saginaw Methodist Church addition°	Saginaw
	Defoe house°	Bay City
	Standolin Gas and Oil alternative to standard house°	
	First Methodist Church	Midland
	Northeast Intermediate School	Midland
1949	Lape apartments°	
	Hoobler house	Ann Arbor
	Phoenix Civic Center	Phoenix, AZ
	St. John's Episcopal Church	Midland
1950	Ballmer house	Midland
	Friselle house	Midland
	Harrington cottage°	Indian River
	Bulmer house°	
	Colpaert house°	South Bend, IN
	Fountain Street Baptist Church°	Grand Rapids
	Elks clubhouse°	Midland
	Lapelle's Flow Shop remodeled	Midland
	Meyers house	Lapeer
	G. Duffy house	Port Huron
	Ward house°	Big Rapids
	R. Bennett house	Midland
1951	Yates house	Midland
	Comey house	St. Clair Shores
	Bay County recreation shelter°	
	Alliance Clay Products office°	Alliance, OH
	Bergstein house	Midland
	Ashmun house	Midland
	Housing project°	
	University of Michigan Margaret Bell Pool	Ann Arbor
	Athay house	Midland
	James house	Midland
	Sutton house	Midland
	Plymouth Elementary School	Midland
1952	Arcade building alteration°	Midland
	Colburn house	Midland
	Sandwich house°	Midland
	Defoe house	Bay City
	Goldberger house	Saginaw
	LeFevre house°	Midland
1953	St. John's Lutheran Church	Midland
	Messiah Lutheran Church°	Bay City
	MacDonald house°	Ann Arbor
	Grace A. Dow Library	Midland
	Folded plate house°	
	Herbert Dow house	Midland
	Herbert Doan house	Midland
	Community center	Midland
1954	Phoenix Civic Center Museum	Phoenix, AZ
	Evans house°	
	Birmingham house°	Adrian
	Upjohn theater°	Kalamazoo

	Smith's Flower Shop remodeled	Midland
	Senior high school	Midland
	Dow Chemical biochemical research°	Midland
	Midland National Bank	Midland
	Sherk house	Midland
	Nelson Street Elementary School	Midland
1955	Chrysler carousel display	Florida
	Munson house°	Midland
	Ashmun Street Church of God	Midland
	Hotel Chieftan°	Mt. Pleasant
	Harlow house	Midland
	Dick house	Grand Rapids
	A. S. Arbury & Sons office	Midland
	Bay City Jewish Center	Bay City
	Homestyle Center Foundation house	Grand Rapids
	Fire Station #1	Midland
	J. Duffy house	St. Clair Shores
	Midland Country Court House addition	Midland
	Dow Chemical nuclear research°	Midland
	Olson house	Midland
	Skating rink°	Midland
1956	Diplomatic housing compound°	Pasay, Philippines
	Ashmun house revisions	Midland
	Kilian office°	Frankfort
	Consumers Power office	Midland
	Webster house°	Midland
	Herbert Dow cottage	Crystal Lake
	Dow Chemical agricultural chemical research building°	Midland
	Public library	Ann Arbor
1957	Opperman house	Saginaw
	Blackhurst house	Midland
	McMorran Memorial Auditorium	Port Huron
	Marshall house	Midland
	Jewish Center	Midland
	Gable house	Midland
	Ward Memorial Presbyterian Church°	Livonia
	L. I. Doan house	Midland
	First Methodist Church°	Grand Haven
	Post office°	Houghton Lake
	Reed houe	Houston, TX
	Pierson house	Saginaw
	Dow Chemical administration center, central service	Midland
	Consumers Power office	Bay City
	Parkdale Elementary School	Midland
1958	Surath house°	Midland
	Howell house	Midland
	Christ Episcopal Church	Adrian
	Control tower°	Cottage Grove

151

Project Drawings

	Grebe house°	Midland
	Reorganized Church of Latter Day Saints addition	Midland
	Kings Daughters Home	Midland
	Miner S. Keeler II house	Grand Rapids
	Community center	Ann Arbor
	Hillsdale College dining hall	Hillsdale
	Schuette house	Midland
	Rowland house	Midland
1959	Cannon house°	Mona Lake
	Eastminster Presbyterian Church°	East Lansing
	Freligh house	Adrian
	Interlochen girls dormitory	Interlochen
1960	Collinson house	Midland
	Washburne house	Okemos
	Blackhurst Realty°	Midland
	Davis house	Mt. Pleasant
	Leonard Refineries service station	Midland
	Mid-Michigan Broadcasting Station°	
	Crown Petroleum service station°	Bay City
	Hrobon house°	Columbus, OH
	Emry/Kraus houses	Mt. Pleasant
	Allen house addition°	Midland
	Holy Family Episcopal Church°	Midland
	Kalamazoo Christian Church°	Kalamazoo
	Salvation Army building°	Midland
	Oberlin house°	Massillon, OH
	Hillsdale College girls dormitory	Hillsdale
	University of Michigan Botanical Gardens Superintendent house	Ann Arbor
	Interlochen master plan	Interlochen
1961	Clinic°	Kalamazoo
	Hunter house°	Midland
	Roscommon Congregational Church	Roscommon
	Branch house	Midland
	Ballman house (Stein) addition	Midland
	Bay Refining service station	Midland
	Reicker house	Midland
	Laird house°	Ann Arbor
	Senior high school°	Meridian
	Interlochen classroom #1	Interlochen
	Saginaw Valley College Somnaphonic Garden°	
	Ann Arbor City Hall	Ann Arbor
	Jamieson house	East Tawas
	McMorran Arena	Port Huron
	Chestnut Hill School addition°	Midland
1962	A. B. Dow house door°	Midland
	Temple Beth El	Spring Valley, NY
	House Beautiful lanterns°	
	Salvation Army "Citadel"°	Midland
	Conductron Corporation offices	Ann Arbor

	Elementary school addition°	Mapleton
	Midland National Bank	Midland
	Carras house	Midland
	Interlochen gymnasium,, science #1	Interlochen
	Northwood Institute dining hall, dormitory, classroom	Midland
	Regina High School°	Midland
	Nazarene Church	Midland
	Jefferson Intermediate School	Midland
1963	Greek Orthodox church	Pontiac
	First Presbyterian church°	Alma
	Duke University president's house	Durham, NC
	People's National Bank°	Bay City
	Townsend house	Bloomfield Township
	Beth Israel community center°	Ann Arbor
	Morris house°	Ann Arbor
	Northwood Institute site lighting	Midland
	Interlochen language arts	Interlochen
	Hillsdale College student center	Hillsdale
	Kalamazoo Nature Center	Kalamazoo
	Seventh Day Adventist Church	Midland
	Alumni living building°	Ann Arbor
	Mapleton High School°	Mapleton
1964	First Methodist Church°	Lansing
	Hellenic Orthodox church	Bloomfield Township
	Birmingham-Bloomfield Bank°	
	Lutheran church office	Ann Arbor
	Gerstacker house addition	Midland
	Northwood Institute faculty housing	Midland
	Interlochen dormitory, Kresge Auditorium, store	Interlochen
	YWCA	Saginaw
	Hillsdale College Olds Dormitory addition	Hillsdale
	University of Michigan Institute for Social Research, theater, botanical gardens	Ann Arbor
	Phoenix Civic Center museum addition	Phoenix
	Saginaw Valley College administration student union, master plan	
	Tri-City Airport	
1965	Markley house°	Bloomfield Hills
	D. R. Bennett house°	Midland
	Drapery designs°	
	University Microfilms	Ann Arbor
	Interlochen boys dormitories	Interlochen
	Hillsdale College Strosaker Science Center	Hillsdale
	Muskegon County Community College	Muskegon

Saginaw Valley College master plan
   (Brysellebout, Dow, Wigen)
University of Michigan Towsley   Ann Arbor
   Center for Continuing Medical
   Education
Wayne State University physical   Detroit
   education facility°

1966 Junior Achievement Center°   Midland
Ypsilanti Greek Theater°   Ypsilanti
Ramada Inn°   Midland
Northwood Institute°   Cedar Hills, TX
Bloomfield Hills Country Day   Bloomfield Hills
   School°
University of Michigan   Ann Arbor
   administration offices
Northwood Institute fraternity, Midland
   student activities, union
Dow Chemical office, 2030 Abbot Midland
   Rd.
Muskegon County Community   Muskegon
   College gymnasium
H. H. Dow High School   Midland
Wayne State University, University Detroit
   Center

Hillsdale College nursery   Hillsdale
Northern Michigan University   Marquette
   Learning Resources
Church & Guisewite office building Midland
1967 First Church of the Nazarene° Southfield
Livonia City Hall°   Livonia
Greenhills school   Ann Arbor
Muskegon County Community   Muskegon
   College Fine Arts
Mary Dow house   East Lansing
Chemical Bank   Midland
Professional building°   Mt. Pleasant
Central Michigan Inn pro shop° Mt. Pleasant
Bay Refining service station   Midland
Plymouth Park city pool   Midland
Mid-Michigan Community College
   instructional facility
Delta College classrooms
Saginaw Valley College
   instructional facility #1,
   dormitory village #1, library
Interlochen library   Interlochen
Cleveland Manor   Midland

Index

Numbers in italic indicate illustrations.

Sidney K. Robinson is on the faculty of Iowa State University at Ames. He received his doctoral degree in architecture from the University of Michigan. He is co-author of a monograph on the Prairie School in Iowa, published in 1977, and author of several articles in architectural journals.

The manuscript was edited by Jean Owen. The book was designed by Edgar Frank. The typeface for the text is Autologic APS-5 Highland. The display face is Autologic APS-5 Optimist. The book is printed on 80-lb. Mead Moistrite Matte paper. The hardcover edition is bound in Holliston Mills Zeppelin cloth over binder's boards. The paperback edition is bound in Riegel's Carolina Cover CIS.

Manufactured in the United States of America.